# THE BLACK ISRAELITE
# EXODUS
## AT THE END OF THE AGE

## An Exegesis of the Prophecy of Genesis 15:12-14

**Revealing the hidden Israelite identity of Black People in the 400 Year African Diaspora and discussing their destined role in the events leading up to the Second Coming of Christ**

### IWEZE SHARIEFI BEN ABUDU

ISBN 978-0-578-36813-9 (pbk)

Cover design (front) & Daniel Statue artwork (p. 93) by Cleveland Palmer & Iweze Ben Abudu. Cover photo (back) courtesy of Getty Images.

Published by:

EXODUS COMMITTEE

***Peace & Love from Iweze***

*To The Twelve Tribes of Israel*
*Scattered Abroad*

*And to My Beloved Brothers and Sisters*
*In Christ Jesus (Yahushua Hamashiac)*

# TABLE OF CONTENTS

# PREFACE

**Iweze, a servant of God and the Lord Jesus Christ (Yahushua Hamashiac), greetings to the Black people of the United States of America in the Four Hundred-Year Sojourn brought about by the Transatlantic Slave Trade.**

I have written this book because the present time necessitates it. The prophetic keys of eschatology handed down to us throughout biblical scripture unlock the reality that we have now transitioned into the last days of this present age. Therefore, it is essential that during this time, we come to the collective realization and understanding that we are a special people who have been chosen by God and who have a divine prophecy to fulfill. Ultimately, this prophecy's final fulfillment will liberate us from our four hundred year period of affliction, in this land not our own, and lead us back into the Land of Promise. Unfortunately, however, us being in the Diaspora, enduring through slavery, and being subjected to years of systematic deception and repression have severely obscured these facts. Nonetheless, I have hope that in reading this book, not only will you get a clear understanding of our true identity and the prophecy we are to fulfill but that you will also be able to utilize this book as a lens or framework to **1)** conduct further research **2)** to stimulate organization and **3)** to mobilize when called upon to do so by God himself.

Before reading the remainder of this book, you must be made aware of the basic premises forming its foundation. They are the following: **1)** Biblical *"scripture is given by inspiration of God, and is profitable for doctrine, for reproof, for correction, for instruction in righteousness: that the man of God may be perfect"* (2 Timothy 3:16-17)

1

**2)** The Bible, in most cases, should be interpreted literally and accepted as real history (e.g., Eve being fashioned from Adam's rib by God (Gen. 2:21-23), Moses dividing the Red Sea with his staff (Ex. 14:21), Jesus being born of a virgin and rising from the dead on the third day (Mat. 1:22-23, Acts 2:23-24) should all be taken literally) **3)** The symbolic passages of the Bible, such as those written in the books of Daniel and Revelation, represent real events that have or will take place **4)** Prophecy is a real phenomenon (2 Peter 1:19-21) and **5)** The coming of our Lord and Savior Jesus Christ (Yahushua Hamashiac) is close at hand! Anyone subscribing to these same views must take the arguments and conclusions of this book very seriously.

Finally, although this book points out some harsh realities that we in the Diaspora have been subjected to for four hundred years by people primarily of white European descent, by no means is it the intention of this book to sow racial discord within the body of Christ and among various persons of goodwill. On the contrary, like Paul, I recognize and affirm that our struggle ultimately transcends flesh and blood and that *"we wrestle against principalities, against powers, against the rulers of the darkness of this world, against spiritual wickedness in high places"* (Ephesians 6:12). Having said this, may the words on the following pages be an eternal blessing to you all.

**Your Faithful Servant
In Christ Jesus (Yahushua Hamashiac),
Iweze**

# INTRODUCTION

**And when the sun was going down, a deep
sleep fell upon Abram; and, lo, an horror
of great darkness fell upon him. And he
[YAH] said unto Abram, Know of a surety
that thy seed shall be a stranger in a land
that is not theirs, and shall serve them;
and they shall afflict them four hundred
years; And also that nation, whom they
shall serve, will I judge: and afterward
shall they come out with great substance
(Genesis 15:12-14, KJV)**

Besides the Bible, you may have read or heard about
the above prophecy in whole or in part from many other
sources. For example, placing the prophecy's fulfillment
within a Europeanized ancient Egyptian context, Cecil B.
Demille's epic film *The Ten Commandments* (1956) has
undoubtedly played no small role in propagating the
vision's message:

> (Film Excerpt 1)
> **Moses:** That's a hard dance you do old man.
> **Simon:** We've been dancing it for four hundred
> years...
> **Mered:** And the only deliverer that has come to
> us is death.
> **Taskmaster:** Back to work, you braying mules!

> (Film Excerpt 2)
> **Joshua:** But why are you dressed as a slave?
> Why does a Prince of Egypt kill the Pharaoh's
> Master Builder to save a Hebrew?
> **Moses:** I am Hebrew.
> **Joshua:** God of Abraham. Four hundred years
> we have waited...

**Moses:** The guards won't wait so long!
**Joshua:** The Almighty has heard our cries from bondage. You are the chosen one![1]

Following the same interpretive tradition as Demille, the more recent film *Exodus: Gods and Kings* (2014) has spread the "four hundred years of Egyptian bondage" concept to a younger generation:

> (Film Excerpt)
> **Moses:** It's not easy to see the people who I grew up with suffering this much.
> **Malak:** What about the people you didn't grow up with? What thought did you give to them? You still don't think of them as yours, do you? As long as Rhamses has an army behind him, nothing will change.
> **Moses:** Anything more is just revenge!
> **Malak:** Revenge? After 400 years of brutal subjugation! These pharaohs, who imagine they're living gods, they are nothing more than flesh and blood! I want to see them on their knees begging for it to stop![2]

On a less spectacular scale, but no less significant, an abundance of written commentary has weighed in over the centuries regarding the prophecy, the majority of which place the prophecy's fulfillment within an ancient Egyptian context as well. And within the Black community itself, many Black leaders and Black preachers have spoken of a four hundred year Egyptian bondage in their speeches and sermons. However, for their part, some have taken note of how well the prophecy parallels and appears to describe the experiences of Black people here in Ameri-

---

[1] *The Ten Commandments.* Dir. Cecil B. Demille. Paramount Pictures, 1956. Film.
[2] *Exodus: Gods and Kings.* Dir. Ridley Scott. 20th Century Fox, 2014. Film.

ca. After all, we were brought to a land not our own as strangers, were forced into slavery and servitude, and have been afflicted (oppressed) for the past four hundred years.[3]

However, despite the striking similarities between our experiences and the events foretold in Abraham's prophecy, the vast majority of Black people in America have not overcome centuries of misleading indoctrination to draw a definite conclusion that the prophecy refers to us. Instead, many have fallen prey to the mainstream consensus that the ancient Israelites fulfilled the prophecy in Moses' day.

Regardless, the prophecy of Genesis 15:12-14 does indeed refer to our four hundred year plight here in the United States of America. And understanding this fact reveals the mystery of our true identity as being not only the descendants of Abraham but also the direct descendants of the Twelve Tribes of Israel. It also reveals our ultimate destiny of leaving America with great substance (wealth) and going back to our original homeland of Israel once judgment comes to our oppressors.

Therefore, this book's first objective is to prove the veracity of these claims by primarily exposing the false notion that the ancient Israelites had been afflicted for four hundred years before the Exodus out of Egypt. The fact of the matter is, if we carefully scrutinize the scriptures without the influence of preconceived notions, it should come into plain view that Israel's bondage in Egypt only lasted about eighty years and does not meet the full criteria of Abraham's nightmarish vision. It should also come into view that we, the Black people of America, are the only people throughout the whole of world history who meet the criteria of the prophecy of Genesis 15:12-14 and that the day of our liberation is now at hand!

The second objective is to show how the prophecy of Genesis 15:12-14 is an end-time prophecy whose final fulfillment will take center stage in a series of apocalyptic

---

3 Early 1600's to Present = Approximately 400 years.

events leading up to the coming of our Lord and Savior Jesus Christ (Yahushua Hamashiac).

# CHAPTER 1
## Four Hundred and Thirty Years
## In Egypt Debunked

$A$lthough both are incorrect, two prevailing interpretations exist throughout the world today regarding the fulfillment of Abraham's four hundred year prophecy. Of the two, the more widely accepted interpretation posits that it was fulfilled during a four hundred and thirty-year sojourn of Israelites in Egypt in accordance with the rendering of the following verse:

> **Now the sojourning of the children of Israel, who dwelt in Egypt, was four hundred and thirty years. (Exodus 12:40, KJV translation of Masoretic Text)**

The other viewpoint quarrels with the idea that Israel sojourned in Egypt for such a considerable length of time by attributing the first half of the four hundred and thirty years to the patriarch's sojourn in Canaan. It goes on to argue that the four hundred years of affliction began during the early childhood years of Isaac and ended with the Exodus out of Egypt (see Chart 1 on page 8). Despite the wide popularity, however, of the first position, it is far more erroneous than this latter one, which we will now turn to see.

The Masoretic[1] rendering of Exodus 12:40 (above) used in most Protestant Bibles is, in essence, a faulty transmission of the original Hebrew account that has been left uncorrected throughout the years. Moreover, the error has grossly allowed ancient Egypt to be considered a candidate for the entire fulfillment of Genesis 15:12-14. Whereas, the

---

[1] Copied and edited between the 7th and 10th centuries, the Masoretic Text (MT) is a Hebrew text of the Tanakh (Old Testament) approved for general use in Judaism.

# Chart 1

**View 1**

## 430 Years in Egypt

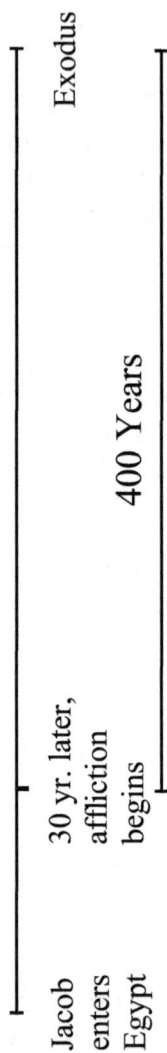

Jacob enters Egypt

30 yr. later, affliction begins

400 Years

Exodus

**View 2**

## 215 yrs in Canaan + 215 yrs in Egypt

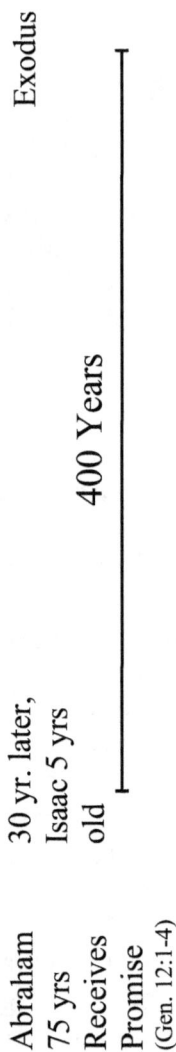

Abraham 75 yrs Receives Promise (Gen. 12:1-4)

30 yr. later, Isaac 5 yrs old

400 Years

Exodus

8

# Chart 2

## Patriarchs' Sojourn In Canaan

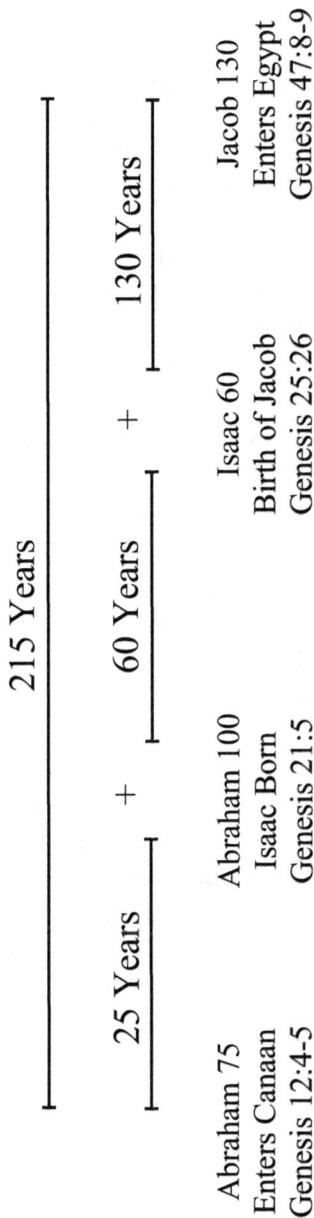

215 Years

25 Years  +  60 Years  +  130 Years

Abraham 75
Enters Canaan
Genesis 12:4-5

Abraham 100
Isaac Born
Genesis 21:5

Isaac 60
Birth of Jacob
Genesis 25:26

Jacob 130
Enters Egypt
Genesis 47:8-9

215 yrs in Canaan + 215 yrs in Egypt = 430 Year Sojourn

original and uncorrupted Hebrew account of the verse when translated reads like this:

> **Now the sojourning of the children of Israel *and of their fathers* which they had dwelt *in the land of Canaan and* in Egypt was four hundred and thirty years. (Based on original Hebrew)**

Notice here that this rendering of Exodus 12:40 divides the four hundred and thirty years between the time the patriarchs spent in Canaan and the time Israel spent in Egypt. Furthermore, because it is easy to calculate the length of time the patriarchs sojourned in Canaan using the book of Genesis, which was two hundred and fifteen years (see Chart 2 on page 9), it is easy to determine the correct amount of time Israel spent in Egypt as well. The ancient Israelites only sojourned in Egypt for two hundred and fifteen years, making it impossible to squeeze a four hundred year prophecy into a two hundred and fifteen-year context. With this in mind, one can already begin to see the grave error made by Viewpoint #1 and how we must not "throw the baby out with the bath-water" concerning Viewpoint #2, for therein are some things worth salvaging.

Nonetheless, to validate the claims made up to this point, we will examine the testimony of not just two or three witnesses, which, according to the Bible, is sufficient enough to establish a matter (Deuteronomy 19:15). Instead, six witnesses will now be presented, followed by a seventh witness in the next chapter.

# Witness 1:
## The Lineage of Kohath ben Levi

**The sons of Levi; Gershon, Kohath, and Merari. And the sons of Kohath; Amram, Izhar, and Hebron, and Uzziel. And the children of Amram; Aaron, and Moses, and Miriam...(1 Chronicle 6:1-3)**

From the above passage, as well as from Exodus 6:16-20 and Numbers 26:57-59, it is revealed that the lineage of Kohath leading down to Moses at the time of the Exodus is far too short to fit within a four hundred and thirty year context. Kohath, who was numbered among the seventy or so souls that went down into Egypt with Jacob (see Genesis 46 & Acts 7:14), was only Moses' grandfather. To get a full grasp of how short of a time-frame this reality suggests, consider how Abraham was Kohath's great-great-grandfather (Abraham>Isaac>Jacob>Levi>Kohath). And given that from Abraham's entrance into Canaan down to Jacob, Levi, and Kohath's entrance into Egypt fits within a two hundred and fifteen-year context, as was shown earlier, there is no way that from Kohath's entrance into Egypt down to his grandson Moses at the time of the Exodus can fit within a four hundred and thirty-year context. Kohath, Amram, and Moses did not live longer than Abraham, Isaac, and Jacob (and Levi). It was the the other way around, as shown below:

| | |
|---|---|
| **Abraham** | 175 years (Genesis 25:7) |
| **Isaac** | 180 years (Genesis 35:28) |
| **Jacob** | 147 years (Genesis 47:28) |
| **Levi** | 137 years (Exodus 6:16) |
| | VS. |
| **Kohath** | 133 years (Exodus 6:18) |
| **Amram** | 137 years (Exodus 6:20) |
| **Moses** | 120 years (Deuteronomy 34:7) |

## Witness 2:
## Paul's Epistle to the Galatians

The Apostle Paul's epistle to the Galatians also contains a truth lying in plain sight for determining the actual length of Israel's sojourn in Egypt. However, it is often glanced over or turned a blind eye to due to the mental blockage the Masoretic account of Exodus 12:40 tends to cause. In Galatians 3:16-17, Paul confirms that the four hundred and thirty-year sojourn was not just limited to Egypt, but also encompassed the time the patriarchs spent in Canaan. It states,

> **Now to Abraham and his seed were the promises made. He saith not, And to seeds, as of many; but as of one, And to thy seed, which is Christ. And this I say, that the covenant, that was confirmed before of God in Christ, the Law, which was four hundred and thirty years after, cannot disannul, that it should make the promise of none effect.**

When Abraham entered the land of Canaan at seventy-five years old and had received the promises and the covenant (see Genesis 12:1-7, 15:18), Paul tells us in the above passage that the Law came four hundred and thirty years later. In other words, Paul is saying that the four hundred and thirty years spoken of in Exodus 12:40 really cover the time from when Abraham entered into Canaan down to the Exodus, at which time the Law was given. Now, let's pause here to ponder an apparent contradiction. Either Paul's assessment of the four hundred and thirty years is correct and the notion that Israel spent four hundred and thirty years in Egypt is wrong, or Paul is wrong and the notion that Israel spent four hundred and thirty years in Egypt is right, but they both cannot be true at the same time. Based on the testimony of books in the Bible that record the short lineage of Kohath down to Moses showing that Kohath was Moses' grandfather, it is safe to conclude that Paul is right and that the Israelite sojourn in Egypt was only half of the four hundred and thirty years. But rather than just deducing the shorter time-frame of Israel's sojourn in Egypt from our first two witnesses, there are other ancient documents, translations, and biblical manuscripts that actually preserve the original message of Exodus 12:40 so that we can be certain about the conclusions drawn thus far. The witnesses which follow will demonstrate how this is so.

## Witness 3:
## The Septuagint

With Greek being used internationally during the early formation of the Christian Church, the Septuagint (LXX)—the most ancient Greek translation of the Hebrew Old Testament[2]—came to be relied on by the early Church. It also best matches the majority of Old Testament quotations found in the New Testament (see Chart 3 on page 14). Concerning Paul's understanding of the geographical context for the four hundred and thirty-year sojourn (i.e., Canaan & Egypt), we find, like the many OT quotations, that it too is wholly consistent with the Septuagint. In Exodus 12:40, the LXX states,

> **And the sojourning of the children of Israel, while they sojourned in the land of Egypt and the land of Chanaan, was four hundred and thirty years.**

---

[2] The Septuagint's origins date back to the reign of Ptolemy II Philadelphus king of Egypt (285-246 BC) who first commissioned the work.

**Chart 3:** Manuscript Comparison Examples

| MASORETIC | SEPTUAGINT | NEW TESTAMENT |
|---|---|---|
| **Isaiah 7:14**<br>"Therefore the Lord himself will give you a sign. Look, the young woman [Heb.-almah] is with child and shall bear a son, and shall name him Immanuel." | **Isaiah 7:14**<br>"Behold, a <u>virgin</u> [Gr.-Parthenos] shall conceive in the womb, and shall bring forth a son, and thou shalt call his name Emmanuel." | **Matthew 1:23**<br>"Behold, a <u>virgin</u> [Gr.-Parthenos] shall be with child, and shall bring forth a son, and they shall call his name Emmanuel." |
| **Psalm 40:6**<br>"Sacrifice and meal offering You have not desired; My ears You have opened; Burnt offering and sin offering You have not required." | **Psalm 40:6**<br>"Sacrifice and offering thou wouldest not; but <u>**a body hast thou prepared me**</u>: whole-burnt-offering and sacrifice for sin thou didst not require." | **Hebrews 10:5**<br>"Sacrifice and offering You have not desired, <u>**But a body You have prepared for Me**</u>" |
| **Deuteronomy 21:23**<br>"If a man has committed a sin worthy of death and he is put to death, and you hang him on a tree, his corpse shall not hang all night on the tree, but you shall surely bury him on the same day (for he who is hanged is accursed of God)" | **Deuteronomy 21:22-23**<br>"And if there be sin in any one, and the judgment of death be upon him, and he be put to death, and ye hang him on a tree: his body shall not remain all night upon the tree, but ye shall by all means bury it in that day; <u>for every one that is hanged on a tree is cursed of God</u>" | **Galatians 3:13**<br>"Christ redeemed us from the curse of the Law, having become a curse for us—for it is written, <u>**Cursed is everyone who hangs on a tree**</u>" |

14

From this passage, it is plain to see that when the Apostle Paul penned Galatians 3:16-17, he was not speaking in some loose or general sense of time that would appear to contradict holy writ. Instead, the LXX passage above shows Paul spoke with a high degree of precision that failed to make its way into the Masorete copy of Exodus 12:40 for one reason or another.

## Witness 4:
## The Samaritan Torah

Another useful tool of textual criticism relating to the topic at hand comes to us by way of the Samaritans. This small community, consisting today of just a few hundred souls, still worships upon Mount Gerizim near Nablus (biblical Shechem) with the doctrine of the Woman at the Well, who conversed with Jesus (see John 4:20). The Torah preserved among them (Samaritan Torah/Pentateuch) is in a Samaritan script akin to Paleo-Hebrew—the script used in ancient Israel before the Babylonian captivity. It also contains some differences with the Masoretic Text, with a number of those differences agreeing with the Septuagint. Regarding this ancient text's Exodus 12:40, however, it goes a step further than the Septuagint by providing an even smoother and more thorough account therein. It states,

> **Now the sojourning of the children of Israel *and of their fathers* which they had dwelt in the land of Canaan and in Egypt was four hundred and thirty years.**

The few extra details this passage provides over its Septuagint counterpart (i.e., children of Israel + and of their fathers) serve to present us overall with the best reflection of the historical reality the Apostle Paul alluded to in Galatians 3:16-17. They also present us with what is

Fig. 1, Samaritan High Priest and Old Pentateuch. Keystone View Company, 1905. Stereograph In Views of Palestine (1905). The J. Paul Getty Museum.

perhaps the closest depiction of what the original Hebrew version of Exodus 12:40 may have looked like when it was first written, especially when viewed in the Samaritan script itself.

## Witness 5:
## Titus Flavius Josephus
## (Yosef Ben Matathiyah)

Following the four biblical sources (i.e., Kohath's lineage, Galatians, Septuagint, and Samaritan Torah) that attest to the shorter duration of time Israel spent in Egypt, we will now turn to Josephus' testimony. He was a descendant of the priest-kings that ruled Israel before the rise of the Herodian Dynasty. He also was a contemporary of Paul and the other Apostles. Eventually, he rose to head Israel's forces in Galilee during what is known as the First Jewish-Roman War. During the time of the Temple's destruction by the Romans around 70 AD, Josephus was given leave by Titus Caesar to retrieve the holy books of Israel,[3] which he most likely used to write his *Antiquities of the Jews*. In his book, Josephus had this to say about the four hundred and thirty years:

> **They left Egypt in the month of Xanthicus, on the fifteenth day of the lunar month; four hundred and thirty years after our forefather Abraham came into Canaan, but two hundred and fifteen years only after Jacob removed into Egypt.[4] (Book 2, 15:2)**

---

3 The Life of Flavius Josephus, sec. 75.
4 Like many, Josephus appears to have struggled with finding the proper context for the prophecy of Genesis 15:12-14 (see Book 2, 9:1) and assigned it to Egypt, while at the same time acknowledging here that Israel sojourned in Egypt for only two hundred and fifteen years.

Josephus makes it abundantly clear what the traditional understanding of Exodus 12:40 was among the Israelites up to his day.

## Witness 6:
## William Whiston

Given the testimonies of the witnesses mentioned thus far, the false notion that Israel spent four hundred and thirty years in Egypt should be plain to see, along with the erroneous association of Abraham's four hundred year prophecy with a context half its time. In finishing up our treatment of Viewpoint # 1, however, it is worth mentioning that the Old Testament's Masorete copy should not now be spurned. For all of the significant extant manuscripts have their unique value and work collaboratively with one another to help compensate in those areas where one of them falls short. Nonetheless, regarding the Masoretic text's Exodus 12:40, it is most appropriate to end this segment of our discussion with the following quotation taken from William Whiston—the 18th-century translator of the writings of Josephus into English:

> **Why our Masorete copy so groundlessly abridges this account in Exodus 12:40, as to ascribe 430 years to the sole peregrination of the Israelites in Egypt when it is clear even by that Masorete chronology elsewhere, as well as from the express text itself, in the Samaritan, Septuagint and Josephus, that they sojourned in Egypt but half that time, -and that by consequence, the other half of their peregrination was in the land of Canaan, before they came into Egypt, -is hard to say. (Antiquities of the Jews Book 2, Ch. 15:2 footnote)**

18

Whatever the correct answer is to Whiston's question above remains a mystery, which is perhaps less important than recognizing the error, along with the overall negative effect the Exodus 12:40 abridgment has had on millions throughout many generations. Nevertheless, just as we have separated fact from fiction regarding Israel's sojourn in Egypt, let us now turn to uncover the facts as to why viewpoint # 2 is not a viable alternative or prospect for the fulfillment of Abraham's prophecy as well.

# CHAPTER 2
## Touch Not My Anointed

In response to the obvious dilemma presented with trying to superimpose a 400-year prophecy onto a 215-year context, some have still tried to assign Abraham's prophecy to that distant past by forcefully incorporating the sojourn in Canaan into the equation. Instead of seeking out a better alternative, many go back four hundred years before the Exodus out of Egypt to the days of Isaac's early childhood, desperately searching for anything that might resemble the prophecy's criteria. In being dissatisfied with going away empty-handed, Ishmael's mockery of his little brother Isaac[1] is then offered up as the starting point for four consecutive centuries of oppression by foreigners who afterward would be judged. The fact that Ishmael's offspring were never the recipients of Moses' ten plagues is of little or no importance to them. Some then cite Joseph's thirteen-year trial in Egypt as part of the affliction despite the record showing that he went on afterwards to rule over Egypt for the next eighty years (Genesis 41:39-46, 50:26). The challenges and shortcomings of the pre-Exodus[2] approach toward understanding the prophecy of Genesis 15:12-14 should be coming into plain view with just the small amount of commentary provided thus far.

Now, the patriarchs were not exempt from the occasional misfortunes all men under the sun have had to endure. However, by taking a sound approach toward analyzing the times in which they lived, one shouldn't view the patriarchal period in Canaan, and even a good portion of the sojourn in Egypt, as a time of affliction. Contrarily, this period should be seen as a time of divine protection,

---

[1] Genesis 21:9

[2] Before the exodus out of Egypt is what I mean here and elsewhere within this chapter.

favor, and great glory. Therefore, the remainder of this chapter will serve to highlight this fact, as well as to provide some clarification on key aspects of Israel's history prior to them leaving Egypt.

## Witness 7:
## Psalm 105:8-15

One of the most excellent illustrations that capture the essence of how blessed and safeguarded the patriarchs were before Israel's trials in Egypt comes down to us through a psalm of King David. An excerpt from it reads as follows:

> He hath remembered his covenant for ever, the word which he commanded to a thousand generations. Which covenant he made with Abraham, and his oath unto Isaac; And confirmed the same unto Jacob for a law, and to Israel for an everlasting covenant: Saying, Unto thee will I give the land of Canaan, the lot of your inheritance: **When they were but a few men in number; yea, very few, and strangers in it. When they went from one nation to another, from one kingdom to another people; He suffered no man to do them wrong: yea, he reproved kings for their sakes; Saying, Touch not mine anointed, and do my prophets no harm.**

This description of the patriarchs' wanderings in Canaan is quite the opposite of what Abraham's nightmare describes (i.e., slavery, affliction, and being humbled 400 years). According to this passage, the patriarchal period was undergirded with a "touch not my anointed" decree that the highest earthly authorities could not violate. In less abstract terms, this time was marked with the likes of Abraham's victory over the kings of the east (Genesis 14),

Pharaoh's punishment in the affair concerning Sarah (Genesis 12:17), Abimelech king of Gerar entreating Isaac for peace (Genesis 26:26-30), and Israel's slaughter of the Shechemites after the defilement of Dinah (Genesis 34). And though the children of Israel were few in number, their reputation was such that as they journeyed, scripture says, *"the terror of God was upon the cities that were round about them, and they did not pursue after the sons of Jacob"* (Genesis 35:5). Such was the glory of the patriarchs in Canaan and is in no way comparable to the prophecy of dire straits revealed unto Abraham.

Now, unbeknownst to many because of the confusion surrounding the issues at hand is the fact that the same favor Israel enjoyed in the land of Canaan also extended into the greater part of their two hundred and fifteen-year sojourn in Egypt. For instance, it took time for the children of Israel to go from the small number of about seventy-five souls in Egypt (Acts 7:14) to becoming the strong multitude the Egyptians became afraid of and tried to repress (Exodus 1:7-10). In fact, by taking scripture at face value, we learn that it was only somewhere near the last eighty years of Israel's dwelling in Egypt that they spent under the yoke of oppression. This figure is derived by factoring in Moses' age at the time of the Exodus (80 yrs; Exodus 7:7) with the fact that he was born during the reign of the pharaoh that first began Israel's mistreatment (Acts 7:18-20). Ironically, Israel's liberator was adopted into this same pharaoh's household once he was discovered floating in the river as an infant by Pharaoh's daughter (Exodus 2:1-10, Acts 7:18-21). Nevertheless, Israel prosperously sojourned in Egypt for well over a hundred years before the coming of that new king who "knew not Joseph" and wore Israel down ($\approx$135 yrs + $\approx$80 yrs = 215 yrs).

From a broader historical perspective encompassing the entire 430 years of Exodus 12:40, the following overview is now given: From Abraham's sojourn in Canaan to Jacob and his sons' entrance into Egypt in the 9th year of Joseph's rule, was 215 years. Seventy-one years later, Joseph died at the age of 110. Afterward, Egyptian goodwill towards Israel continued for no more than 64 years when a new king who knew not Joseph began to afflict Israel. At this time Moses was born, being the seventh generation from Abraham and the fourth generation from Levi.[3] 80 years after Moses' birth, and in the 215th year after Israel first went down into Egypt (71 + ≈64 + ≈80 = 215), the Exodus occurred.

At this point, it should be safe to say that a pre-Exodus approach for identifying the fulfillment of Genesis 15:12-14 has been proven to be thoroughly unsound. The chronological record and the collective testimonies of six key witnesses attest that the children of Israel were not in Egypt long enough to meet the 400-year requirement. And a seventh witness reveals the error of using the patriarchs' sojourn in Canaan to solve that problem.

Nonetheless, given that there is no evidence of the prophecy's fulfillment before the Temple's destruction in 70 A.D., one is forced to look for that reality within the unfolding drama of Israel's nearly two thousand year dispersion throughout the nations. For some, such a task might present itself as a bit of a challenge, especially given that Satan has endeavored viciously to hide Israel's true identity from the world, and even from Israel itself. However, if done in the spirit of truth and with the Holy Spirit's aid, one would ultimately discover that the experiences of Black people in the United States of America match the prophecy's criteria like no other people in history.

---

3 Three separate topics are covered in God's vision to Abraham in Genesis 15:13-16, which are 1) 400 years of affliction of Abraham's seed 2) Abraham dying at a good old age in peace and 3) A four-generation circumstance Abraham's descendants would undergo, i.e., from Levi's entrance into Egypt down to Moses and the Exodus.

# CHAPTER 3
## Questions and Answers

Despite the arguments and analyses provided thus far, which leave us in the Four Hundred Year African Diaspora as the sole candidates for the fulfillment of Genesis 15:12-14, a few more questions may still need answering before the implications of such a reality are entirely realized and accepted. Therefore, this chapter aims to address a variety of curiosities and concerns that have surfaced around the news of a Black Israelite Exodus destined to soon take the world by storm.

**Question 1:** **What other factors may have led scholars to wrongfully link Abraham's prophecy to that generation of Israelites who came out of Egypt with Moses?**

**Answer:** One apparent reason scholars have connected the prophecy with the Egyptian enslavement of Israelites is the following: After being presented with the prophecy in the book of Genesis, the reader is quickly presented with a description in Exodus that resembles the prophecy's criteria.[1] As a result, the reader's mind instantly links up the vision with the Egyptian enslavement without paying close attention to the critical details that reveal to us that such a link should not be made.[2] Perhaps, however, if Abraham's prophecy were not exposed to the reader ahead of time, one would be inclined to look deeper into that particular history to figure out the correct length of time the Israelites were enslaved and oppressed in Egypt.

[1] The ancient Israelites in Egypt were indeed enslaved and afflicted in a land that was not their own, but not for four hundred years.
[2] The reader makes the same cognitive mistake in reading Acts 7 concerning the prophecy and the enslavement in Egypt.

Moreover, some scholars have failed to realize, or keep in mind, that scriptures were written very cleverly and that drawing sudden conclusions can result in crucial mistakes, especially if the subject matter is the interpretation of prophecy and its fulfillment. For example, **the nature of Scripture is such that when a prophecy is given, events are sometimes provided soon afterward that give the appearance of being the fulfillment of the prophecy, but are not the actual fulfillment.** Not only is this the case with Genesis 15:12-14 and the enslavement of Israelites in Egypt, but this can also be seen with some of the events that took place after Daniel prophesied. For example, many scholars had mistakenly concluded that the prophecy of Daniel 9:24-27 was ful-filled during the Persian and Greek periods when the Sec-ond Temple of Jerusalem was built and then polluted with the emergence of Antiochus Epiphanes3 (see Ezra 1 & 1 Maccabees 1:54). However, Yahushua (Jesus) pointed out that the fulfillment of Daniel's prophecy would take place during the days of Great Tribulation at the end of this present age (Matthew 24:15-21). Thus, even though the Temple's rebuilding followed by its pollution in the days of Antiochus both appeared to be a fulfillment of Daniel 9:24-27 by meeting some of the prophecy's criteria, they were not the actual fulfillment. In the same way, even though the Israelite enslavement in Egypt appeared to be a perfect fulfillment of Genesis 15:12-14 by meeting some (not all) of its criteria, it was not the actual fulfillment.4

Another key factor contributing to a misunderstanding of the timing of the four hundred years prophecy is that it represents only one layer of a three-layered message given to Abraham all at once. Each of these layers was meant to

---

3 Antiochus Eiphanes (a Seleucid king) had set up an appalling abomination in the Jewish Temple at Jerusalem during the Macca-bean period (read 1 Maccabees 1:54 & 2 Maccabees 6:1-5).
4 This dynamic is also at work in Isaiah 7:10−8:4 concerning the fu-ture child to be born.

be viewed in their own separate and distinct setting, but given the form in which they were delivered and recorded in Scripture, many readers have gotten tripped up. Let's take a look at this three-layered message to Abraham:

**(Layer 1)**
**Ge 15:12 And when the sun was going down, a deep sleep fell upon Abram; and, lo, an horror of great darkness fell upon him. Ge 15:13 And he said unto Abram, Know of a surety that thy seed shall be a stranger in a land that is not theirs, and shall serve them; and they shall afflict them four hundred years; Ge 15:14 And also that nation, whom they shall serve, will I judge: and afterward shall they come out with great substance.**

**(Layer 2)**
**Ge 15:15 And thou shalt go to thy fathers in peace; thou shalt be buried in a good old age.**

**(Layer 3)**
**Ge 15:16 But in the fourth generation they shall come hither again: for the iniquity of the Amorites is not yet full.**

As one can see, these three layers appear to have some continuity between them, especially between layers 1 & 3 in that they both address the children of Israel. However, on a deeper level, they discuss the children of Israel at different points in time, which is where much confusion is generated. It has already been shown how Layer 1 does not fit with Israel prior to the departure out of Egypt, while Layer 3 is a reference to the Egyptian experience and subsequent conquest of the land of Canaan. The four generations of verse 16 refer to the days of Levi (1), Kohath (2), Amram (3), and Moses (4). However, without carefully and "rightly dividing the word of truth," one can easily associate this four-generation period of two hundred and fifteen years with the four-hundred-year prophecy directly before it.⁵ In terms of Layer 2, it is a reference to Abraham's own life span.

Nonetheless, the layering method, as exemplified above, is one that is very common to the spirit of prophecy, which weaves in and out of both the present and the future whensoever it pleases. Moreover, to further demonstrate this phenomenon with the hope of not being superfluous, here is another example taken from Genesis 3:14-16:

> Ge 3:14 And the LORD God said unto the serpent, Because thou hast done this, thou art cursed above all cattle, and above every beast of the field; upon thy belly shalt thou go, and dust shalt thou eat all the days of thy life:
>
> ***Ge 3:15 And I will put enmity between thee and the woman, and between thy seed and her seed; it shall bruise thy head, and thou shalt bruise his heel.***
>
> Ge 3:16 Unto the woman he said, I will greatly multiply thy sorrow and thy conception; in sorrow thou shalt bring forth children; and thy desire shall be to thy husband, and he shall rule over thee.

The italicized portion of this passage (v. 15), abruptly shifts the time reference away from what was taking place in the immediate between God and the serpent (v. 14), to a

---

5 Biblical numerical-generations are based on lineage. See also Matthew 1:1-17.

drama of spiritual warfare that would begin to unfold long afterward as outlined in Revelation 12 (see also Rev. 13:3). Verse 16 (above) then picks back up where verse 14 leaves off in time. However, if one were not careful, one could easily miss this layering in God's discourse and misinterpret it through the wrong perspective of time, just as many have done with the four-hundred-year prophecy.

Finally, with any prophecy whose fulfillment is far into the future by hundreds or even thousands of years, it should be no surprise that interpretive mistakes would come before the appointed time. Furthermore, because many Bible scholars are liable to make mistakes that are detrimental to our understanding of the truth that the Bible so wonderfully reveals, **we must take the time out to carefully read the ENTIRE Bible for ourselves.** By doing this, we will be able to learn what is in the scriptures for ourselves and be able to call all of its scholars and teachers to a higher standard of accuracy and truthfulness.

**Question 2: How is it possible for the Black people of America, who are in the Four Hundred Year African Diaspora, to be Israelites given that the Israelites or Jews are predominantly a white-skinned people?**

**Answer:** For quite some time now, the world has been led into believing that the children of Israel are primarily white-skinned people when nothing could be further from the truth. The physical descendants of the original Israelites are people of color (i.e., Black people), and the Bible, as well as secular sources, give us a sufficient amount of evidence proving this to be the case. To begin our exploration, let us journey back to the land of ancient Egypt when the children of Israel sojourned there for two hundred and fifteen years and grew into a great nation.

Fig. 2. Giza Pyramids & Sphinx - Egypt. Image by Nadine Doerlé (2010) from Pixabay

The book of Exodus records Israel's last eighty years in Egypt,[6] which took place within the Nineteenth Dynasty, also known as the Ramesside period.[7] However, much of the hundred and thirty-five years preceding this time would have taken place during the second half of the Eighteenth Dynasty, from which some of Egypt's most well-known pharaohs emerged (e.g., Tuthmosis III, Queen Tiye, Akhenaten and Nefertiti, Tutankhamun). Joseph, who would have ruled in his day alongside the pharaohs down in Thebes (Waset)—the Egyptian capital during much of the Eighteenth Dynasty—was given the daughter of the priest of On (Heliopolis) for his wife (Genesis 41:45). Together they became the progenitors of two tribes in Israel (Ephraim and Manasseh). Moreover, based upon numerous archaeological findings and the testimony of ancient writers and historians (e.g., Herodotus, Diodorus Siculus, Ammianus Marcellinus, etc.), the natives of Egypt (biblical Mitzraim) were black[8]—a fact that certainly would have rubbed off on Joseph's half-Egyptian children. The Egyptians being black is also a fact worth keeping in mind when seeing how Joseph's brothers could not recognize him as being one of their own upon their entry into Egypt (Genesis 42:8). Could Joseph have been mistaken for being a black Egyptian? If so, he certainly didn't hold exclusive rights preventing such a phenomenon from occurring

---

6 This time spans from the birth of Moses, who was born during the reign of the pharaoh who began Israel's affliction, down to the Exodus.

7 Scripture says "they built for Pharaoh treasure cities, Pithom and Raamses" (Exodus 1:11). By the reign of Merneptah (son of Raameses II), Israel had gone out of Egypt according to the Merneptah Stele.

8 According to Herodotus (c. 484 BC - c. 425 BC), "the natives [of Egypt] are black because of the hot climate" and like the Colchians "have black skins and wooly hair" (*The Histories* 2:22 & 2:104). Diodorus Siculus (c. 90 BC - c. 30 BC): "They say also that the Egyptians are colonists sent out by the Ethiopians, Osiris having been the leader of the colony" (Book 3, ch. 3). Ammianus Marcelinus (c. 330 AD - C. 395 AD): "Now the men of Egypt are, as a rule, somewhat swarthy and dark of complexion" (Ammianus, Book 22:16:23).

Fig. 3. North Side of the West Wall of Nakht's (18th Dynasty official buried at Thebes) Offering Chapel. 2-dimensional 1 to 1 Copy. Norman de Garis Davies - 1915 for Metropolitan Museum in New York.

to other high profile Israelites; for such was the case with Moses, who had taken unto himself an Ethiopian wife (Numbers 12:1), and with the Apostle Paul. Scripture says the following about these two spiritual giants:

## Moses

"Now the priest of Midian had seven daughters: and they came and drew water, and filled the troughs to water their father's flock. And the shepherds came and drove them away: but Moses stood up and helped them, and watered their flock. And when they came to Reuel their father, he said, How is it that ye are come so soon to day? And they said, **An Egyptian delivered us out of the hand of the shepherds**..." (Exodus 2:16-19).

## Paul

"And as Paul was to be led into the castle, he said unto the chief captain, May I speak unto thee? Who said, **Canst thou speak Greek? Art not thou that EGYPTIAN,** which before these days madest an uproar... But Paul said, I am a man which am a Jew" (Acts 21:37-39).

If you will notice here in Paul's mistaken identity case, being a Jew was closer in terms of appearance to the Egyptian race than it was to the Greek race. Paul's race was practically indistinguishable from that of a native Egyptian and is perhaps why some of the ancient Gentile writers easily conceived of the notion that the entire nation of Israel was Egyptian in origin. The Greek geographer Strabo (64 or 63 B.C. – c. A.D. 24), for example, remarked thus concerning Israel:

The Jews have places assigned them in Egypt, wherein they inhabit, besides what is peculiarly

33

allotted to this nation at Alexandria, which is a large part of that city. There is also an ethnarch allowed them, who governs the nation, and distributes justice to them, and takes care of their contracts, and of the laws to them belonging, as if he were the ruler of a free republic. In Egypt, therefore, this nation is powerful, because **the Jews were originally Egyptians,** and because the land wherein they inhabit, since they went thence, is near to Egypt. (Strabo quoted in Josephus' *Antiquities of the Jews*, Book 14, Chapter 7)

Nevertheless, the ancient Egyptians were not the only people of color the children of Israel were identified with in antiquity. According to the Roman senator and historian Tacitus[9] (c. 56 - c. 120 A.D.), many in his time imagined the Jews to be a race of Ethiopians, as is written below:

As I am about to relate the last days of a famous city, it seems appropriate to throw some light on its origin. Some say that the Jews were fugitives from the island of Crete, who settled on the nearest coast of Africa about the time when Saturn was driven from his throne by the power of Jupiter. Evidence of this is sought in the name. There is a famous mountain in Crete called Ida; the neighbouring tribe, the Idaei, came to be called Judaei by a barbarous lengthening of the national name. Others assert that in the reign of Isis the overflowing population of Egypt, led by Hierosolymus and Judas, discharged itself into the neighbouring countries. **The greatest part, however, say that they were a race of Ethiopian origin,** who in the time of King Cepheus were driven by fear and hatred of their neigh-

9  It was this Tacitus who left us a remarkable testimony concerning our Lord and Savior ("Christus") and the Christians who are named after him (Tacitus, *Annals*, 15:44).

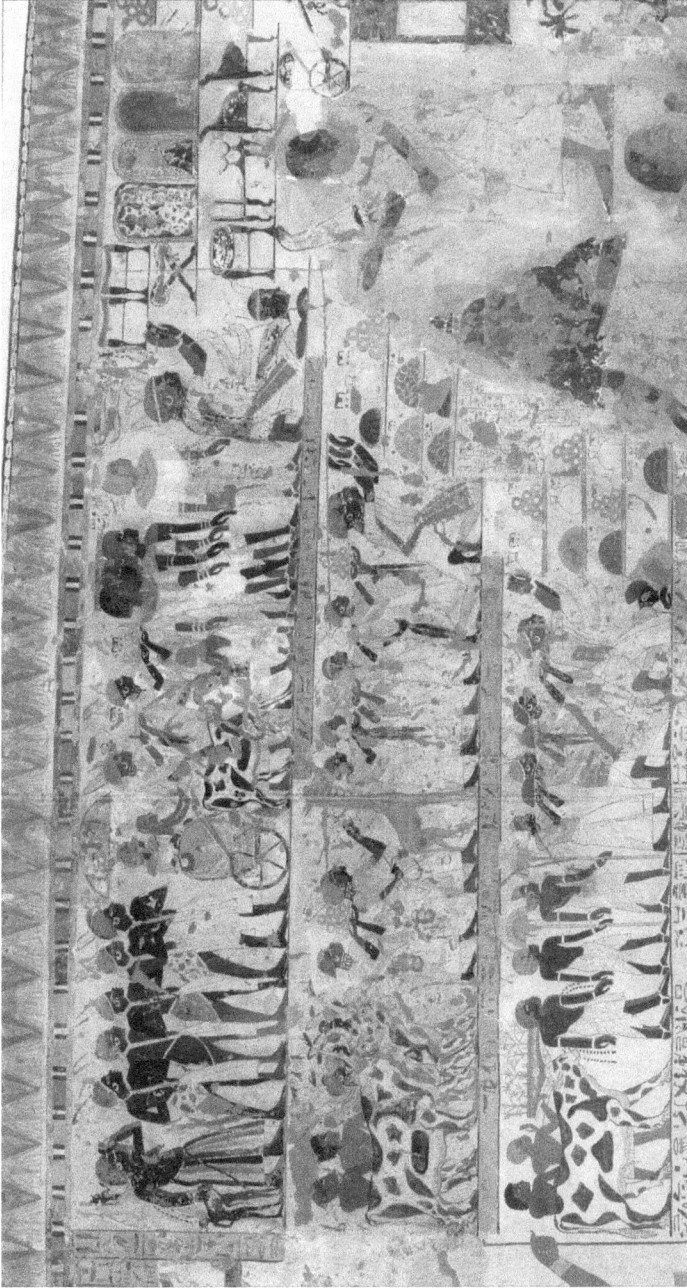

Fig. 4. Nubian (Ethiopian/Cushite) Tribute Presented to the King, Tomb of Huy (reign of Akhenaten–Tutankhamun 18th Dynasty). Facsimile. Charles K. Wilkinson, 1923–27. Metropolitan Museum.

bours to seek a new dwelling-place. (Tacitus, *The Histories*, Book 5.2)

Although Tacitus' passage displays some confusion many had regarding Israel's real history, the revelation that Israel was a black nation screams through it loud and clear. It would have been silly for a man of Tacitus' learning and eminence within the Roman power structure to relate the possibility of Israel being a race of Ethiopians if they didn't look the part in the eyes of Tacitus' audience. Regardless, they most certainly looked the part in the eyes of the Most High when he stated in Amos, *"Are ye not as children of the Ethiopians unto me, O children of Israel? Saith the Lord. Have not I brought up Israel out of the land of Egypt?"* (Amos 9:7).

Nevertheless, aside from the evidence presented thus far giving a glimpse of Israel's physical appearance, the smoking gun in our discourse here is the sure word of prophecy. Through the prophecy of Genesis 15:12-14, Israel can be identified definitively. And the only people who meet the prophecy's criteria are the Black people of America in the four hundred year Diaspora brought about by the Trans Atlantic Slave Trade. The prophecy is a mirror for the "African American" experience. Our final fulfillment of it will set the record straight once and for all to the surprise of many and the chagrin of others the world over.

**Question 3: If the original Israelites are black, where do the "white Jews" come from, and how are they viewed within the grand scheme of things?**

**Answer:** Despite the white Jews' claim of being descendants of the original Israelites, the reality is that they are no such thing. While the ancient Israelites and their modern-day descendants are Black people, as was just discussed, many trace the origin of the "white Jews" back to Eastern Europe and the ancient kingdom of the Khazars.

# Fig. 5. Map Depicting
## General Location of Ancient Khazaria

Fig. 5. Map Depicting General Location of Ancient Khazaria

Khazaria was located just north of the Caucasus Mountains in what is now western Russia (see map on page 37). Around *"740 A.D., the king, his court, and the military ruling class embraced the Jewish faith, and Judaism became the state religion of the Khazars."*[10] However, this initial embracing of Judaism represented only one phase in their conversion process. *"A generation or two after the conversion there was a reformation of religion under their king Obadiah, when synagogues and schools were built and the Khazars became familiar with Torah, Mishnah and Talmud and with the liturgy."*[11] Eventually, Judaism became so deeply embedded amongst the Khazars that their adherence to this religion was maintained amongst the significant number of Khazars that had migrated into other East and Central European lands before and after the collapse of their state. Initially, some of those lands included Hungary, Poland, Lithuania, and the Balkans, which, in addition to the Khazars' land of origin (now Russia), cultivated and produced most white so-called Jewry one sees today.

Moreover, out of the midst of white European nationalism, imperialism, colonialism, and the European scramble for Africa, the Middle East and a variety of other lands, came to birth the Zionist movement in the late 1800s. By that time, white so-called Jews had dwelt all over Europe but often found themselves alienated from their host countries. And rather than setting their hearts on a national homeland in Europe to solve their problems, the so-called Jews promulgated the lie through Zionism[12] that they were the descendants of the original Israelites and set out to conquer the land of Israel as if they were the true heirs to that land.

---

[10] Koestler, Arthur. *The Thirteenth Tribe*, p. 15.

[11] Dunlop, D.M. *The History of the Jewish Khazars.* Princeton, N.J.: Princeton University Press, 1954, p. 148.

[12] **Zionism:** The secular and political movement of white so-called Jews to deceptively take over the land of Israel.

With the publishing of the Zionist manifesto entitled, *Der Judenstaat* (German for, *The Jew's State*) in 1896 by the Hungarian born so-called Jew Theodore Herzl (1860-1904), and with the emergence of the Zionist Congress with Herzl as its first president, Zionism had reached a significant turning point in its development. Herzl worked to place his Zionist scheme on the imperialistic list of any major European power that had the capacity and willingness to support a so-called Jewish settlement in Israel under the protection of that European power. By doing this, the Zionists hoped to create a scenario that would allow continuous waves of so-called Jewry to settle in Israel with protection and without inhibition so that in the long-run, their increasing numbers would be enough in the region to set up a Zionist state. Herzl did not live long enough to see this scheme manifest.

Nevertheless, the British (who had previously taken part in the Berlin Conference (1884-1885) to further sanction the carving up of Africa into a political jigsaw puzzle) finally realized that the Zionists could be used strategically as instruments of their own imperial and colonial ambitions. At the outset, the British sought to place the so-called Jews in places such as Egypt and East Africa or other British possessions that were not yet inhabited by white settlers. However, the Zionists rejected these proposals and kept the land of Israel as their primary and only target for conquest.

It wasn't until the outbreak of World War I that the British saw the real benefits of establishing a protectorate over a Zionist territory in Israel. The British needed to create a stronghold in the region to protect their control of the Suez Canal from attack, as well as to protect their other interests in the Middle East, and a British protectorate over a Zionist territory in Israel would fulfill those needs. Therefore, a quid pro quo deal was struck between the British and the Zionists (1917). The British were able to have their stronghold over Israel using a friendly subject people, and the Zionists got the protectorate that they were looking for, which would allow their immigration plans to go forward.

However, as time went on and as new interests began to develop for the British, especially with their Arab "friends" in oil-rich territories in the Middle East, Zionist interests changed. They no longer viewed the British mandate over Israel as an asset. The Zionists realized that the British had become a barrier to their immigration plan. The British had hampered immigration of so-called Jews into Israel to appease their Arab friends who were against it. As a result, three years after World War II, the Zionists defeated the British to gain independence and declared such in 1948. This declaration of independence and the establishment of the Zionist State in Israel officially solidified the Zionist Lie. Although the Zionists were not authentic Jews, they had succeeded in appropriating both the identity and the national homeland of the original black Twelve Tribes of Israel.

Unfortunately, many have not been able to shake off the Zionist delusion and have come to view the creation of the Zionist state as the fulfillment of Bible prophecy regarding Israel's restoration in the last days. However, Scripture is very clear that Israel's restoration will truly be a miraculous event like what the world witnessed when the children of Israel left out of Egypt, if not more spectacular. The prophecy of Genesis 15:12-14 reveals this fact through its parallels to what took place in Egypt, and other restoration prophecies give us the same similarities as well. For example, here is what the prophet Ezekiel wrote concerning the restoration:

> As I live, saith the Lord GOD, surely with a mighty hand, and with a stretched out arm, and with fury poured out, will I rule over you: **And I will bring you out from the people, and**

Fig. 6. David Ben-Gurion (First Prime Minister of Israel) publicly pronouncing the Declaration of the State of Israel, May 14 1948, Tel Aviv, Israel, beneath a large portrait of Theodor Herzl, founder of modern political Zionism. Photo by Rudi Weissenstein. Courtesy of Israel Ministry of Foreign Affairs.

**will gather you out of the countries wherein ye are scattered, with a mighty hand, and with a stretched out arm, and with fury poured out. And I will bring you into the wilderness of the people, and there will I plead with you face to face. Like as I pleaded with your fathers in the wilderness of the land of Egypt, so will I plead with you, saith the Lord GOD.** And I will cause you to pass under the rod, and I will bring you into the bond of the covenant: And I will purge out from among you the rebels, and them that transgress against me: I will bring them forth out of the country where they sojourn, and they shall not enter into the land of Israel: and ye shall know that I am the LORD. (Ezekiel 20:33-38)

Ezekiel's mentioning of God gathering Israel with a stretched out arm and fury poured out (compare to Deut. 4:34), bringing Israel back into the wilderness (compare to Ex 5:1), pleading with Israel face to face (compare to Ex 20:22, 33:11), bringing Israel under the Covenant (compare to Ex 24:7), and purging the rebels out prior to Israel entering into the land (compare to Numbers 32:13) are things Israel and the world have not seen since the days of Moses.

The Zionist movement, on the other hand, was driven more by a secular impetus whose essence is perhaps best captured by the following passage taken from the Zionist's ("Israeli") declaration of independence (1948):

**The state of Israel will... ensure complete equality of social and political rights to all its inhabitants irrespective of religion, conscience, language, education and culture; it will safeguard the Holy Places of all religions; and it will be faithful to the**

**principles of the Charter of the United Nations."**[13]

How different this Zionist statute is, compared to the following Covenant decrees ordained in the Torah:

> **You shall have no other gods before me. You shall not make unto thee any graven image, or any likeness of any thing that is in heaven above, or that is in the earth beneath, or that is in the water under the earth: You shall not bow down yourself to them, nor serve them: for I the LORD thy God am a jealous God... (Exodus 20:3-5)**

> **When the Lord your God shall bring you into the land where you go to possess it, and have cast out many nations before you... You shall destroy their altars, and break down their images, and cut down their groves, and burn their graven images with fire. (Deuteronomy 7:1-5)**

Zionism obviously falls short of what is to be expected from the last days' restoration of Israel—a fact that many of the so-called Jews' own rabbis have acknowledged. However, the Zionist phenomenon is not without its place in Bible prophecy, as the following prophecy of Noah delineates:

> **And he said, Blessed be the Lord God of Shem; and Canaan shall be his servant. God shall enlarge Japheth, and he shall dwell in the tents of Shem; and Canaan shall be his servant. (Genesis 9:26-27)**

---

13 Article 1 of the Charter of the United Nations encourages the respect of all religions.

In this prophecy, Noah anticipated the land of Canaan being conquered by the nation of Israel, who are of Shem's bloodline (Genesis 17:8). He also anticipated a time of weakness in Israel's history that would allow for Japhet's children to subdue and occupy the land of Israel, which the Zionist state currently manifests. But as the prophecy speaks of Japhet dwelling in tents belonging to Shem, we know that the real owners must rise again to reclaim what is rightfully theirs; and that time has finally come upon us.

**Question 4: It is no mystery that our current Diaspora was brought about by the Transatlantic Slave Trade. However, as modern-day Israelites, how did we get from Israel to Africa in the first place?**

**Answer:** Our initial entrance into Africa came about primarily by way of Northeast Africa.[14] At Israel's southwestern border is the land of Egypt, and just as it did before Israel's conquest of Canaan, the proximity of the two lands naturally allowed for a colorful relationship afterward (Genesis 12:10, 41:44, 42:1-3). For example, King Solomon in his day, who had allied with the powerful Egyptian kingdom by marrying Pharaoh's daughter (1 Kings 3:1), had merchants down in Egypt bringing up linen, horses, and chariots as part of his vast trade network (2 Chronicles 1:16-17). Roughly four centuries later, Jerusalem fell to the Babylonians, and the turmoil that followed compelled many Jews to go down into Egypt as refugees (Jeremiah 43:1-7). The Egyptian cities of Tahpanhes, Migdol, Noph (Memphis), and the region of Pathros (Upper Egypt) all had Jews dwelling in their midst at this time (Jeremiah 44:1).

When Israelite exiles were finally allowed to return to Judea and Jerusalem at the dawn of the Persian world

---

14 Some argue that Israel is part of North-East Africa given that part of Israel is on the African tectonic plate.

empire (Ezra 1:1-5), many chose to stay behind in the lands that they had grown accustomed to; and Israelites living in Egypt were no exception. An Israelite temple that had been located down in Elephantine near Egypt's border with Nubia, and where Elephantine Jews worshipped Yah, reveals just how settled in some Jews were before and during Persian (Achaemenid) rule of Egypt.

By the time the Greeks came to rule over Egypt near the close of the 4th century B.C., the Israelite dispersion had begun to swell quite significantly there. 120,000 Israelites were brought into Egypt as slaves by Ptolemy I, but who were all emancipated by Ptolemy II to secure a translation of the Hebrew scriptures.[15] Alexandria—the capital of Ptolemaic Egypt—became a major Israelite hub and where Israelites exercised quite a bit of autonomy in regulating their civil affairs up to Roman times.

When Roman rule did come to Egypt and much of the Mediterranean world, Philo of Alexandria (c. 20 B.C. – c. 50 A.D.) asserted that at least a million Jews were living within Egypt's borders, as is written below:

> **The city, as the rest of Egypt, has two kinds of inhabitants, us and them, and that there are no less than one million Jews living in Alexandria and the rest of the country, from the steep slope that separates us from Libya to the boundaries of Ethiopia.[16] (Philo, Flaccus)**

Speaking of Libya and Ethiopia (Cush), these lands were not without their fair share of Israelite sojourners. For example, there were devout Jews from the "parts of Libya about Cyrene" present in Jerusalem during the first Christian Pentecost (Acts 2:10). And regarding Ethiopia (Cush),

[15] Josephus, *Antiquities of the Jews*, Book 12, chapter 2.
[16] This sizable Israelite population in Egypt may have been a factor that prompted the LORD to send Joseph, Mary, and Jesus there to avoid the murderous intentions of King Herod (Matthew 2:13-15).

the prophet Isaiah saw a remnant of Israelites that would remain there until the time of the "Second Exodus" when all of Israel will be restored. Isaiah writes,

> And it shall come to pass in that day, that the Lord shall set his hand again the second time to recover the remnant of his people, which shall be left, from Assyria, and from **Egypt, and from Pathros, and from Cush,** and from Elam, and from Shinar, and from Hamath, and from the islands of the sea. And he shall set up an ensign for the nations, and shall assemble the outcasts of Israel, and gather together the dispersed of Judah from the four corners of the earth. (Isaiah 11:11-12)

In a similar vision, the prophet Zephaniah saw dispersed Israelites dwelling even deeper into Sub Saharan Africa. These, he says, would return from *"beyond the rivers of Cush"* to bring the Lord's offering (Zephaniah 3:10).

Nevertheless, when the Temple was destroyed, and Jerusalem fell to the Romans in 70 A. D, the "times of the Gentiles" prophesied by Christ were formally ushered in. His exact words on the subject are as follows:

> **And when ye shall see Jerusalem compassed with armies, then know that the desolation thereof is nigh. Then let them which are in Judaea flee to the mountains; and let them which are in the midst of it depart out; and let not them that are in the countries enter thereinto. For these be the days of vengeance, that all things which are written may be fulfilled. But woe unto them that are with child, and to them that give suck, in those days! For there shall be great distress in the land, and wrath upon this people. And they**

# ISRAEL'S ENTRANCE INTO AFRICA
## (Part of the "Bantu" Migrations)

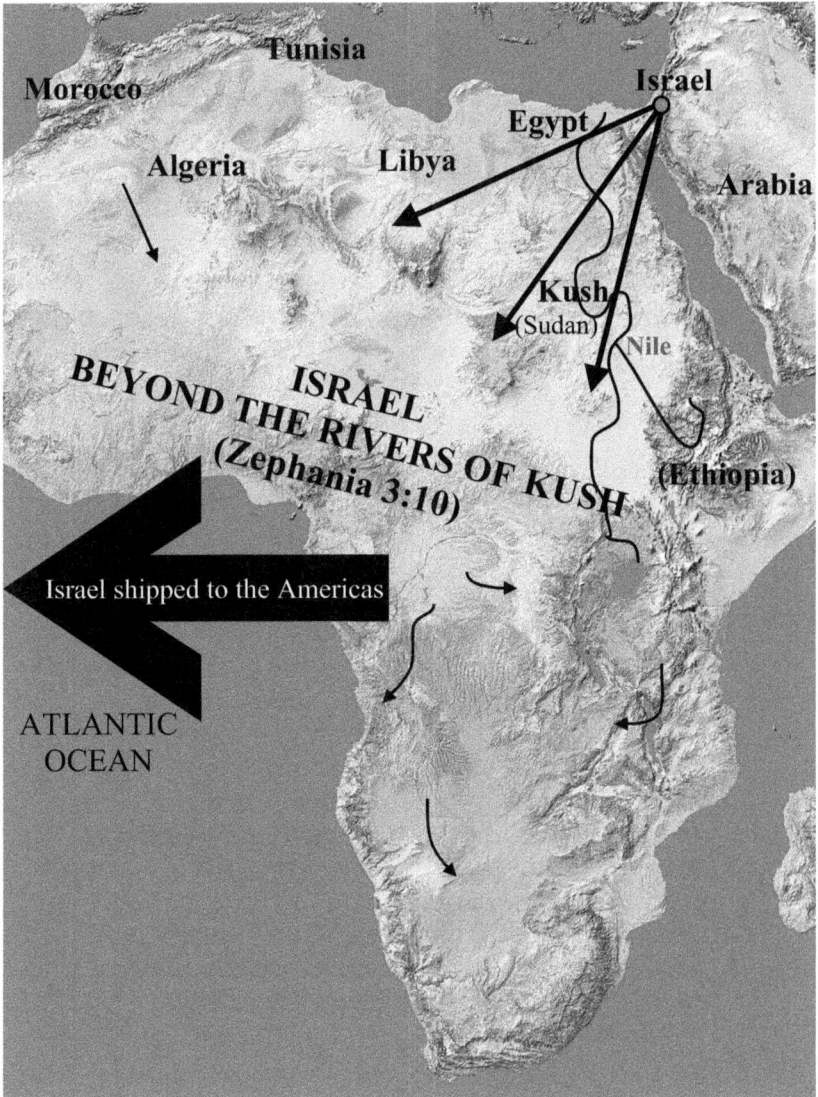

Fig. 7. Israel's Entrance Into Africa.

**shall fall by the edge of the sword, and shall be led away captive into all nations: and Jerusalem shall be trodden down of the Gentiles, until the times of the Gentiles be fulfilled. (Luke 21:20-24)**

Ultimately, with the total loss of our national homeland (Israel and Judah), we had no other option but to adjust and to seek opportunities for our well-being in the lands of our dispersion. Thus, in many ways, our movements in and throughout the African continent were not unlike our migrations throughout America over the years in pursuit of better living conditions. These movements throughout Africa are part of the Bantu migrations. By the sixteenth century A.D., Israelites had become very numerous in Africa. They had migrated and dwelt in a great variety of places throughout the entire continent, especially West Africa as described by Rudolph Windsor below:

> **At the same time that the Jews were migrating westward across the Sudan from Ethiopia, they also migrated southward from Libya, Tunisia, Algeria, and Morocco, to the fertile region between the Senegal and Niger rivers. When the Jews from the north and the east met between these two rivers, they established a confluence or crossroad in West Africa, where men could exchange their culture, ideas, and merchandise. These Jewish migrations went on with great frequency about 300 A.D., and they continued with the utmost regularity for twelve hundred years.[17]**

The rest of our history from this point on is well-known. Through the Trans Atlantic Slave Trade, Israelites in the

[17] Windsor, Rudolph. *From Babylon to Timbuktu*, 1st rev. Edition. Georgia: Windsor's Golden Series, 1988, p. 88-89.

millions were shipped off to the Americas and Europe, where many of us remain unto this day (compare to Deuteronomy 28:68). The prophecy of Genesis 15:12-14 began to be fulfilled when Israelites arrived on Virginia's shores as slaves in the early seventeenth century.

**Question 5: If so-called "African Americans" are Israelites, why is it that most of us don't know our own identity? That is if we are Israelites, wouldn't we know it?**

**Answer:** The greatest factor lending itself to our current state of amnesia regarding our ancient identity is that we were removed far away from our homeland of Israel and dispersed throughout the nations. While dwelling in lands not our own for many centuries, we became vulnerable to **acculturation** and **assimilation** processes, which ultimately gave us new cultural expressions and perspectives.[18]

Whatever remnants of our Israelite identity those processes may have spared during the African phase of our Diaspora, the cruel mechanisms of American slavery[19] wiped them out after a few generations, along with many of the African traditions we had developed or adopted. In replace of these, we adjusted to European culture by adopting their language, attire, personal names, holidays, and even their historical viewpoints. For example, while our own biblical history was being distorted and propagated in the image and interests of Whites and ultimately usurped by them through Zionism, we were taught by Whites that we are Ham's descendants, which is a perception that has long held sway within many Black congregations.

---

[18] Deuteronomy 28:36. See also Daniel 1:3-7, 1 Maccabees 1:1-15, Acts 2:5-11 for how these processes affected Israel in antiquity.
[19] E.g., 1) Separation of members of the same family, tribe, and language 2) Suppression of knowledge and literacy illegality 3) geographic isolation etc.

Nonetheless, because of the confusion stemming from being abroad, many of our people are no longer able to identify themselves as Hebrew-Israelite. Instead, we have been made into what the prophet Ezekiel saw as "dry bones in a valley," or essentially a culturally dead people compared to what we should be (Ezekiel 37:1-14). Fortunately for us, however, this condition is not a permanent one, as Ezekiel would also explain in the following manner:

> **Then he said unto me, Son of man, these bones are the whole house of Israel: behold, they say, Our bones are dried, and our hope is lost: we are cut off for our parts. Therefore prophesy and say unto them, Thus saith the Lord God; Behold, O my people, I will open your graves, and cause you to come up out of your graves, and bring you into the land of Israel. And ye shall know that I am the LORD, when I have opened your graves, O my people, and brought you up out of your graves, And shall put my spirit in you, and ye shall live, and I shall place you in your own land: then shall ye know that I the LORD have spoken it, and performed it, saith the LORD. (Ezekiel 37:11-14)**

**Question 6**: What is the significance of Abraham's four hundred year prophecy given that (A) Israel has been scattered for over two thousand years in many foreign lands and (B) the Transatlantic Slave Trade began over four hundred years ago?

**Answer:** Although Israel has been scattered for over two thousand years throughout the world, Abraham's prophecy represents the last four hundred years of being in such a state. The four-hundred-year timespan is a sign and a countdown clock that indicates when Israel will be restored from the four corners of the earth. It also reveals to us the season in which the days of Tribulation will come upon the world before the coming of Christ, for Israel's restoration marks the beginning of that time. To manifest its signs, the Prophecy singles out a unique and select group of Israelites in the Diaspora that would undergo exactly four hundred long years of affliction by the hands of one particular nation destined for judgment. That nation is none other than the United States of America (the current head of Mystery Babylon). By keeping watch on this context, one would undoubtedly be able to discern the times of change as the four hundred years come to a close.

Moreover, the Four Hundred Year Prophecy is also a roadmap to help guide the Israelites it addresses (so-called "African Americans") back into an awareness of our original identity and purpose after experiencing the most traumatic and culturally disruptive period in our nation's history. By us, the Lost Sheep, perceiving and wrestling with the striking similarities between the prophecy and our own experiences in America, the mystery of our identity is revealed to the end that we might tune up our lives accordingly.

**Question 7:** **What evidence is there aside from slavery that "African Americans" have been oppressed even up to the present?**

**Answer:** Of all the lands that we have been scattered to, none is currently more powerful, more prosperous, and perhaps more vocal in claiming to be a nation promoting freedom, justice, and equality the world over than that of the United States of America. However, beneath the surface of America's boasting, one will find the sad realities of the "African American" experience. While America's founding fathers were busy enshrining the notion that "all

Fig. 8. A family of enslaved Blacks [Israelites] in Georgia, circa 1850.

men are created equal and endowed by the Creator with the inalienable rights of life, liberty, and the pursuit of happiness" (1776), American enslavement of Blacks, already more than a hundred and fifty years old, would push ahead for nearly another century.

## Black Codes & The Era of Jim Crow (the 1860s to the 1960s)

As the dust began to settle from the American Civil War, slavery was finally abolished (except for those convicted of a crime) via the Thirteenth Amendment (1865). Immediately after the amendment's ratification, however, Southern Whites in high positions, and who had not yet gotten over their lust for subjugating Blacks (Israelites), passed a series of *Black Codes* (1865-1866) heavily restricting the freedoms of Black people and creating a context very reminiscent of the antebellum South. Under such laws, Blacks could not gather about freely without having special permission from Whites, were forbidden to own or rent farmland, were forced to work or face imprisonment, and were subject to whippings and a host of other draconian measures. It was an attempt at slavery by other means.

Moreover, concurrent with these laws and times was the emergence of white supremacist groups and organizations like the Ku Klux Klan, who purposed to hinder Black progress up the social, economic, and political ladders by employing tactics of terror, intimidation, and murder.

The ratification of the Fourteenth and Fifteenth amendments (1868 & 1870) attempted to remedy these woes facing Black people by granting citizenship to those born or naturalized in the U.S. (except for American Indians), by granting equal protection under the law, and by giving voting rights irrespective of "race, color, or previous condition of servitude." Civil rights legislation favoring Blacks was also passed in 1875. However, by 1877, a political deal was struck between Republicans (the then party of Lincoln) and Southern Democrats, which gave the South "home rule" and the removal of federal troops from their territory in exchange for giving Republican Rutherford B. Hayes the presidency. This *Compromise of 1877*, as it is called, saw the abandonment of enforcing the new legislation and led to the South having more freedom to craft their own policies for how they would treat Blacks. Birthed from this reality came the era of Jim Crow (1877-1960's).

Now armed with "Home Rule," Southern states, where the majority of Blacks in the U.S. continue to live to this day, began one after another to come up with "Jim Crow" laws of discrimination and racial segregation as a way for Whites to shore up their dominance and sense of "superiority" over Blacks. In this system of American Apartheid, Blacks were relegated to the unequal and inferior "back seats" of society and to the status of being second class citizens. For example, the likes of poll taxes, literacy tests, grandfather clauses, and felony convictions, coupled with violent and deadly intimidation tactics (e.g., lynchings and hangings), circumvented the U.S. Constitution and disfranchised Blacks altogether for years. Moreover, in courts of law, Blacks could not serve as jurors or testify against Whites. Public facilities and accommodations always favored Whites.  On rail cars and buses, Blacks had to sit in the back while Whites sat up front, and if seating was limited, Blacks had to give up their seat to a White person. Public Black schools received far less funding, supplies, and upkeep than White schools did. In "White and Colored" theaters, Blacks had to sit in the balconies. "White and Colored" restaurants partitioned off Blacks away from Whites or made Blacks eat while standing. "White Only" spaces were not to be crossed without being met with severe consequences. After dark, being caught in a White neighborhood could result in being physically attacked, jailed, or murdered. And in terms of

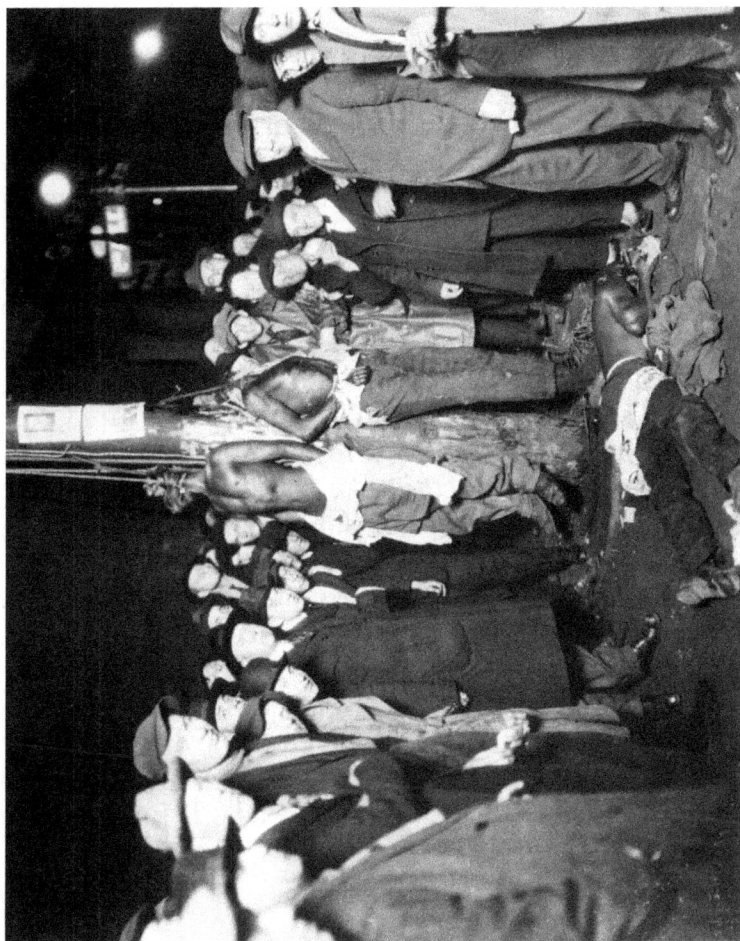

Fig. 9. Lynching of Blacks falsely accused of raping a white woman in Duluth, Minnesota. A June 15, 1920 postcard. Courtesy of Wikimedia Commons.

etiquette, Blacks could be punished for not showing defer-
ence to Whites in the face of being degraded (e.g., White
men were addressed as "Mr." or "Sir" by Blacks, while
grown Black men were addressed as "Boy" in return). All
of this and more were part of the protocols of the Jim Crow
system.

When such social interaction was challenged with the
case of *Plessy v. Ferguson* in the U.S. Supreme Court
(1896), the court decided that laws of racial segregation
were no violation of the U.S. Constitution, so long as seg-
regated facilities had equal standards. This doctrine of
"separate and equal" from America's highest court served
as a nod and a wink for many interested in perpetuating
the oppressive Jim Crow system, which continued to reign
in various ways throughout the United States well off into
the second half of the Twentieth Century.

In 1954, a serious blow was finally dealt to the Jim Crow
Apartheid System with the U.S. Supreme Court case of
*Brown v. Board of Education of Topeka*, in which the
court ruled "that in the field of public education the doctrine of 'separate but equal' has no place. Separate educa-
tional facilities are inherently unequal..." the court stated.
This decision mostly pulled the rug out from under the feet
of *Plessy v. Ferguson* by setting a significant legal prece-
dent used in turn by the Civil Rights Movement to over-
turn apartheid laws in other public arenas. Ultimately, the
Civil Rights Act of 1964, the Voting Rights Act of 1965, and
the Fair Housing Act of 1968 were passed putting a *de jure*
end to Jim Crow.

# 1970's to the present

### The War on Drugs

However, as the end of slavery gave rise to Jim Crow,
this post-Jim Crow era has also presented Blacks (Israel)

with a set of challenges and problems needing to be over-come, some of which continue to afflict our community even unto this day. For example, as the U.S. Government's secret *"Tuskegee Study of Untreated Syphilis in the Negro Male"* (1932-1972) was starting to come to light in the early 1970s, along with the FBI's secret COINTELPRO operations (1956-1971) against Black liberation organiza-tions and personalities (e.g., SCLC and Dr. King, Malcolm X, the Black Panther Party, Fred Hampton, Kwame Ture, etc.), the Nixon Administration (1969-1974) announced a *"War On Drugs"* (1971). For Nixon, however, this war wouldn't squarely be about the drugs. Instead, the war would also be used to go after who he thought was his real domestic enemies in light of the social unrest of the time—Hippies and Black people. Later in a 1994 inter-view, John Ehrlichman—counsel and Assistant to the President for Domestic Affairs under Nixon and a Water-gate co-conspirator—described his former boss' efforts in the following manner:

> **The Nixon campaign in 1968, and the Nixon White House after that, had two enemies: the antiwar left and black peo-ple. You understand what I'm saying? We knew we couldn't make it illegal to be ei-ther against the war or black, but by get-ting the public to associate the hippies with marijuana and blacks with heroin, and then criminalizing both heavily, we could disrupt those communities. We could arrest their leaders, raid their homes, break up their meetings, and vilify them night after night on the evening news. Did we know we were lying about the drugs? Of course we did.[20]**

[20]  Baum, Dan. "Legalize It All: How to win the war on drugs." *Harper's*, April, 2016, pp. 22, 24-34. https://harpers.org/archive/2016/04/legalize-it-all. Accessed 6 Dec.

Moreover, while Nixon was playing his role in the "War on Drugs," the then governor of California, Ronald Reagan (1967-1975), was most likely taking careful notes. When Reagan became president (1981-1989), he doubled down and expanded the "War On Drugs" using similar tactics against Blacks described here by Ehrlichman. For example, under Reagan's watch, a new and inexpensive drug infesting America's inner-cities called Crack Cocaine was criminalized even one hundred times more than its powder equivalent used among Whites and the more affluent. Simultaneously, images of crack mothers and crack babies, who were often portrayed as Black, were being propagated "night after night on the evening news" as a means to justify the raids, arrests, sentencing, and incarceration of Black and Brown drug offenders.

However, one of the most shocking news pieces behind Reagan's "War on Drugs" is that the crack epidemic that first hit during his presidency was being fueled by a CIA backed and funded anti-communist army known as the Contras. According to Gary Webb, a Mercury News staff writer who first broke the story in 1996, members on the CIA's payroll from the FDN (Fuerza Democratica Nicaraguense or Nicaraguan Democratic Force)—the largest of the groups making up the Contras—sold tons of cocaine to U.S. drug dealers (e.g., Freeway Ricky Ross) to raise funds to fight against the socialist Sandinistas who had just taken power in Nicaragua (1979).[21] In assessing the impact this had on Blacks in America, Webb wrote the following:

**"While the FDN's war is barely a memory today, Black America is still dealing with its poisonous side effects. Urban neighborhoods are grappling with legions of**

2019.
[21] The Iran-Contra Affair would also take place during Reagan's presidency.

homeless crack addicts. Thousands of young Black men are serving long prison sentences for selling cocaine—a drug that was virtually unobtainable in Black neighborhoods before members of the CIA's army started bringing it into South-Central [Los Angeles] in the 1980's at bargain-basement prices."[22]

## Black Incarceration

Nonetheless, as the "War On Drugs" continued on after Reagan's presidency in a predominantly punitive manner, and as other "tough on crime laws" were enacted (e.g., Three Strikes, Stop & Frisk, etc.), racial bias, racial disparities, and downright racism embedded within America's criminal justice system have contributed significantly to the issue of Blacks being overrepresented in America's prisons. For example, in 2017, the total adult population in the U.S. was 64% White, 16% Hispanic, and 12% Black. Yet, of those incarcerated in state and federal prisons, 23% were Hispanic, 30% were White, and 33% were Black.[23] It is one thing to have to deal with the just consequences of one's own sin, but to be subject to double standards where Blacks are more likely to be stopped, arrested, convicted, and given longer prison sentences than Whites and others is a problem yet to be rectified.

22  Webb, Gary. "Dark Alliance: America's 'crack' plague has roots in Nicaragua war." *The Mercury News*, Aug. 18, 1996.
23  Gramlich, John. "The gap between the number of blacks and whites in prison is shrinking." Pew Research Center, 30 April, 2019, www.pewresearch.org/fact-tank/2019/04/30/shrinking-gap-between-number-of-blacks-and-whites-in-prison/

## Police Brutality and the Killing of Unarmed Blacks

Moreover, in staying within the realm of law enforcement, police brutality and the unnecessary killing of unarmed (and even legally armed) Blacks are issues that even the world needs no lecture on. Global media is all too familiar with the likes of the beating of Rodney King by LAPD officers (1991); the shooting of Oscar Grant in the back at Fruitvale BART Station by BART Police (2009); the Facebook live-streamed shooting of Philando Castile by a St. Anthony, Minnesota officer (2016); and the strangling of both Eric Garner (by NYPD, 2014) and George Floyd (by Minneapolis P.D., 2020) as they both cried "I can't breathe." Unfortunately, incidences like these have been a constant drip of hostility and injustice towards Blacks (Israelites) for many decades and that no amount of protesting, marching, or rioting have been able to cap off.

Finally, although there are many other issues ill-affecting Blacks that can also be set forth at length, such as: being discriminated against and denied opportunities because of our cultural hairstyles and names; such as Black farmers being denied loans over the years as the Pigford v. Glickman case (1999) has highlighted; such as being the target of hate groups and individuals who commit atrocities like the Charleston Church Massacre (2015) and the lynching of James Byrd, Jr. (1998), etc., we will now conclude this discussion with the hope that what has been set down thus far is sufficient enough to address the topic at hand. We have truly been afflicted in this land not our own for the past four hundred years, and we—the children of Israel—are now ready to enter into the final phase of Abraham's prophecy.

# CHAPTER 4
## Unveiling Prophecy
## From the Black Exodus
## To the Time of the End

According to Bible prophecy, a fixed time period known as the Apocalypse or Great Tribulation will precede the Second Coming of Jesus Christ (Yahushua Hamashiac). No other time in world history will be comparable to it, and if the days of Tribulation were not ordained to be kept short, no flesh, as Christ foretold, would survive (Matthew 24:21-22). But what will be the spark to ignite such an end-time drama shaking both heaven and earth? It is the restoration of the real Twelve Tribes of Israel destined to disrupt the current world order that Satan and his helpers have worked so hard to construct. In fact, the restoration of Israel will be such an affront to Satan's dominion, that his first piece of business upon being cast out of heaven onto the earth will be an unsuccessful attempt to "cut [Israel] off from being a nation; that the name of Israel may be no more in remembrance" (Psalm 83:4). The book of Revelation describes this attempt in this manner:

> And when the dragon saw that he was cast unto the earth, he persecuted the woman which brought forth the man child. And to the woman were given two wings of a great eagle, that she might fly into the wilderness, into her place, where she is nourished for a time, and times, and half a time, from the face of the serpent. And the serpent cast out of his mouth water as a flood after the woman, that he might cause her to be carried away of the flood. And the earth helped the woman, and the

**earth opened her mouth, and swallowed up the flood which the dragon cast out of his mouth. And the dragon was wroth with the woman, and went to make war with the remnant of her seed, which keep the commandments of God, and have the testimony of Jesus Christ. (Revelation 12:13-17)**

The "woman" in this passage is none other than the nation of Israel. The water cast out of the serpent's mouth as a flood represents an international coalition of nations under Satan's influence and command that will be steered to pursue after Israel (compare Daniel 9:26). But just as the earth opened her mouth and swallowed up Korah and his men when they rebelled against Moses and Aaron in the wilderness (Numbers 16), so shall the earth swallow up this contingent of Satan's army. Nevertheless, it is within this apocalyptic framework that the exodus of the prophecy of Genesis 15:12-14 must be viewed, of which the rest of this chapter is dedicated to expounding upon.

### Revisiting the Prophecy of Genesis 15:12-14

And when the sun was going down, a deep sleep fell upon Abram; and, lo, an horror of great darkness fell upon him. And he said unto Abram, Know of a surety that thy seed shall be a stranger in a land that is not theirs, and shall serve them; and they shall afflict them four hundred years; **And also that nation, whom they shall serve, will I judge: and afterward shall they come out with great substance.**

King Solomon wrote in Ecclesiastes 7:8, "Better is the end of a thing than the beginning thereof," and in the case of Abraham's prophecy above, this saying certainly rings true.

After being evil entreated here in the United States of America for four long centuries, this nation, whom we have served, now has a judgment from God pending against her. And just as God's judgment against Egypt and Pharaoh brought about the exodus in the days of Moses, God's judgment against America will have similar results. We will finally leave America with great substance.

## The Coming of Elijah and Moses

Just as our ancestors—the ancient Israelites—had Moses and Aaron lead them out of Egypt, we too will have anointed leaders who will guide us out of America and all the lands of our exile. For example, in the following verses taken from the book of Malachi and the book of Matthew, we are told to expect the coming of Elijah the prophet:

**Malachi 4:5**
**"Behold, I will send you Elijah the prophet before the coming of the great and dreadful day of the LORD."**

**Matthew 17:10-11**
**"And his disciples asked him, saying, Why then say the scribes that Elijah must first come? And Jesus answered and said unto them, Elijah truly shall first come, and restore all things."**

Less conspicuously, Scripture also reveals that Elijah will not be coming alone, but will be accompanied by the prophet Moses of old. In the book of Revelation, for example, it states,

And I will give power unto my two witnesses, and they shall prophesy a thousand two hundred and threescore days, clothed in sack-cloth. **These are the two olive trees, and the two candlesticks standing before the God of the earth**. And if any man will hurt them, **fire proceeds out of their mouth, and devours their enemies:** and if any man will hurt them, he must in this manner be killed. **These have power to shut heaven, that it rain not in the days of their prophecy: and have power over waters to turn them to blood, and to smite the earth with all plagues, as often as they will.** (Revelation 11:3-6)

Although this prophecy does not directly name Elijah and Moses, it indirectly reveals their identity by describing their attributes. For example, we know that in times past, it was Elijah who was given authority to call down fire upon his enemies and to shut heaven for three years and six months so that neither dew nor rain fell (1 Kings 17:1, 18:1, 2 Kings 1:10, James 5:17). And we know that Moses was given authority to turn the waters of Egypt into blood and smite Egypt with all plagues (Exodus 7-12). Furthermore, the imagery and the symbolism of the "two olive trees and the two candlesticks standing before the God of the earth," is reminiscent of Moses and Elijah's appearance before Christ during his transfiguration:

> **And after six days Jesus took Peter, James, and John his brother, and brought them up into an high mountain apart, and was transfigured before them: and his face did shine as the sun, and his raiment was white as the light. And, behold, there appeared**

**unto them Moses and Elijah talking with him. (Matthew 17:1-3)**

Nonetheless, armed with a divine arsenal and tremendous power and authority, Elijah and Moses will not only lead the restoration of Israel but will also preach the pure gospel of the kingdom in all the world for a witness unto all nations (Matthew 24:14). Within three and a half years,[1] the crooked places shall be made straight, and the rough places made plain (Isaiah 40:4), and all of our enemies worldwide will be made low. In fact, it will be during this time that the Antichrist will be slain and his spirit imprisoned in the Bottomless Pit just before his forty-two-month rule, as it is written:

> **And I saw one of his heads as it were slain to death; and his deadly wound was healed: and all the world wondered after the beast... And there was given unto him a mouth speaking great things and blasphemies; and power was given unto him to continue forty and two months. (Revelation 13:3-5)**

> **The beast that thou saw was, and is not; and shall ascend out of the bottomless pit, and go into perdition: and they that dwell on the earth shall wonder, whose names were not written in the book of life from the foundation of the world, when they behold the beast that was, and is not, and yet is. (Revelation 17:8)[2]**

---

[1] 1260 days = 42 months = 3 years 6 months = A time, times, and half a time.

[2] Compare to Louis Farrakhan's predictions about his future absence from the world and his reappearance (e.g., see the last 13 minutes of "Savior's Day 2010: The Wheel" speech). See p. 98 in Suppl.

# 70 Weeks Are Determined
## Until the Coming of the Antichrist

Once we—the armies of Israel—have set the stage for settling our holy city Jerusalem, the following prophecy referred to by Christ (Matthew 24:15) will be awaiting its fulfillment:

> Seventy weeks are determined upon thy people and upon thy holy city, to finish the transgression, and to make an end of sins, and to make reconciliation for iniquity, and to bring in everlasting righteousness, and to seal up the vision and prophecy, and to anoint the most Holy. Know therefore and understand, that from the going forth of the commandment to restore and to build Jerusalem unto Messiah the Prince shall be seven weeks. And threescore and two weeks: the street shall be built again, and the wall, even in troublous times. And after threescore and two weeks shall Messiah be cut off, but not for himself: and the people of the prince that shall come shall destroy the city and the sanctuary; and the end thereof shall be with a flood, and unto the end of the war desolations are determined. And he shall confirm a covenant with many for one week: and in the midst of the week he shall cause the sacrifice and the oblation to cease, and for the overspreading of abominations he shall make it desolate, even until the consummation, and that de-

Fig. 10. Temple Mount, Jerusalem. Image by WerkstattRU (2017) from Pixabay

**termined shall be poured upon the desolate. (Daniel 9:24-27)**

Elijah the prophet (Messiah the Prince) and the Antichrist (prince that shall come) are the two central figures of this prophecy. **It is not until the book of Revelation that we learn from the scriptures that both Elijah and the Antichrist will be coming with partners.** In Elijah's case, he will be accompanied by Moses, as was just shown, and the Antichrist will be accompanied by the False Prophet (Revelation 19:20). Moreover, the coming of these two pairs will be a case of "the good twin versus the evil twin" phenomenon and the world having to choose between the two sides prior to Yahushua's (Jesus') return.

Nonetheless, the seventy weeks here have been divided into three parts: 7 weeks (49 days), 62 weeks (434 days), and 1 week (7 days). During the first 7 weeks and prompted by a royal decree to return, we shall make our way to Jerusalem. During the 62 weeks which follow, parts of the city will be rebuilt (including the Temple, Rev. 11:1-2), and our ancient form of divine service will be reestablished. The holy place will be anointed as in times past, and we shall make national reconciliation/atonement for iniquity (compare Leviticus 16). However, by the final week, Elijah (with Moses) will have finished witnessing and will be killed by the resurrected Antichrist and his forces (see also Revelation 9 & 11:7). Antichrist will then put an end to the divine service and establish himself (the Abomination of Desolation) in the Holy Place (see also Matthew 24:15-21 & 2 Thessalonians 2:3-4), and the period known as the Great Tribulation will have commenced (see Chart 4 on page 69). More regarding this seventieth week is described in the following passage:

> **And when they [Elijah and Moses] shall have finished their testimony, the beast**

68

Chart 4

# Daniel's Prophecy of 70 Weeks
## (Israel's End of the Age Atonement)

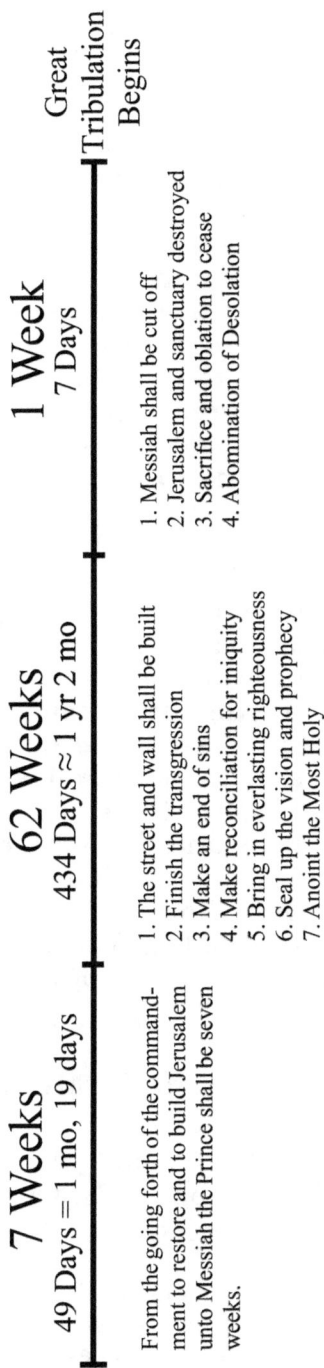

| 7 Weeks | 62 Weeks | 1 Week | |
|---|---|---|---|
| 49 Days = 1 mo, 19 days | 434 Days ≈ 1 yr 2 mo | 7 Days | Great Tribulation Begins |

**7 Weeks**
From the going forth of the commandment to restore and to build Jerusalem unto Messiah the Prince shall be seven weeks.

**62 Weeks**
1. The street and wall shall be built
2. Finish the transgression
3. Make an end of sins
4. Make reconciliation for iniquity
5. Bring in everlasting righteousness
6. Seal up the vision and prophecy
7. Anoint the Most Holy

**1 Week**
1. Messiah shall be cut off
2. Jerusalem and sanctuary destroyed
3. Sacrifice and oblation to cease
4. Abomination of Desolation

* This prophecy will take place during the last 70 weeks of Elijah and Moses' 1260 day ministry.

that ascends out of the bottomless pit[3] shall make war against them, and shall overcome them, and kill them. And their dead bodies shall lie in the street of the great city, which spiritually is called Sodom and Egypt, where also our Lord was crucified [Jerusalem]. And they of the people and kindreds and tongues and nations shall see their dead bodies three days and an half, and shall not suffer their dead bodies to be put in graves. And they that dwell upon the earth shall rejoice over them, and make merry, and shall send gifts one to another; because these two prophets tormented them that dwelt on the earth. And after three days and a half the Spirit of life from God entered into them, and they stood upon their feet; and great fear fell upon them which saw them. And they heard a great voice from heaven saying unto them, Come up hither. And they ascended up to heaven in a cloud; and their enemies beheld them. And the same hour was there a great earthquake, and the tenth part of the city fell, and in the earthquake were slain of men seven thousand: and the remnant were affrighted, and gave glory to the God of Heaven. (Revelation 11:7-8)

## Flee Into the Mountains

Upon witnessing the events pertaining to the Seventieth Week of Daniel's prophecy, Israel must flee immediately into the mountains/wilderness, for Satan will aim to de-

---

3 Killed during Elijah and Moses' ministry, the Beast will ascend out of the bottomless pit and reappear before the world alive. He will in turn kill the two witnesses (See Genesis 3:15).

stroy our nation, as was mentioned at the beginning of this chapter. At that time, *"Let him which is on the housetop not come down to take any thing out of his house: Neither let him which is in the field return back to take his clothes"* (Matthew 24:15-18). Instead, a place has been prepared of God, where Israel will find nourishment and refuge from the face of the serpent for the space of 3 ½ years (Revelation 12:6 & 14).

## War Against Christians

In seeing that he is unable to subdue the tribes of Israel, Antichrist (now at the head of world government) and his armies will turn their attention toward waging a global war against the general body of Christ (non-Israelite Christians):

> **And the dragon was wroth with the woman, and went to make war with the remnant of her seed, which keep the commandments of God, and have the testimony of Jesus Christ. (Revelation 12:17)**

> **And it was given unto him to make war with the saints, and to overcome them: and power was given him over all kindreds, and tongues, and nations. (Revelation 13:7)**

> **And he shall speak great words against the most High, and shall wear out the saints of the Most High, and think to change times and laws: and they shall be given into his hand until a time and times and the dividing of time. (Daniel 7:25)**

It will be during this time that the infamous "Mark of the Beast" system will be implemented so that anyone not willing to worship the Beast (Antichrist) and his image, and anyone not willing to receive his mark in their right hand or in their forehead, are to be killed (Revelation 13:15-18, 20:4). This will be a most grievous time and will require the faith and patience of the saints (Revelation 13:9-10, 14:12). And so shall the state of the Church be *"until the consummation, and that determined shall be poured upon the desolate"* (Daniel 9:27).

## The 7 Last Plagues

After the shedding of much blood (see Rev. 9:18, 12:4), and during the latter part of the Great Tribulation, the LORD, through the following last plagues (see Revelation 15-16), will finally begin to cut short the Kingdom of the Beast and bring it to an end:[4]

**1.** A noisome and grievous sore will fall upon those with the mark of the Beast.
**2.** The sea will turn to blood, and every living soul within it will die.
**3.** The rivers, fountains, and waters will become blood, for as the wicked shed the blood of saints and prophets, they shall be given blood to drink.
**4.** The sun will scorch men with fire and great heat.
**5.** The Beast's kingdom will be filled with darkness, and people will gnaw their tongues for pain and blaspheme the God of Heaven because of their pains and sores.
**6.** Satan, the Beast, and the False Prophet will gather the kings of the earth into Armageddon for the battle of that great day of God Almighty.

---

[4] Trumpets 1-4 (Rev. 8:7-12), America's judgment before the Exodus (Gen. 15:14), and the Beast being mortally wounded (Rev. 13:3) all during Elijah and Moses' ministry foreshadow these 7 last plagues.

**7.** There will be an unprecedented earthquake causing a) the great city (*see Rev. 11:8*) to divide into three parts b) the cities of the nations to fall and c) the islands and mountains to not be found. Mystery Babylon the Great will also be judged,[5] and great hail from heaven will fall upon men.

In these seven last plagues, God's anger will have reached its measure (Revelation 15:1).

**The Coming of Christ
And the Rapture
Of the Dead & Living**

**Immediately after the tribulation of those days shall the sun be darkened, and the moon shall not give her light, and the stars shall fall from heaven, and the powers of the heavens shall be shaken: And then shall appear the sign of the Son of Man in heaven: and then shall all tribes of the earth mourn, and they shall see the Son of Man coming in the clouds of heaven with power and great glory. And he shall send his angels with a great sound of a trumpet, and they shall gather together his elect from the four winds, from one end of heaven to the other.[6] (Matthew 24:29-31)**

---

5  See Revelation 17 & 18 for more on the final judgment of Mystery Babylon the Great. See also *The Mystery of Iniquity Revealed, Part 2* in Supplements.
6  Mark 13:27 states that Christ "will gather his elect from the four winds, from the uttermost part of the earth to the uttermost part of heaven."

Despite the popularity of the doctrine found within many of today's churches that says Christ will gather/rapture his elect before the days of tribulation, the passage above clearly demonstrates how that will certainly not be the case. Instead, *"with a great sound of a trumpet,"* the Church will be gathered *"after the tribulation of those days."*[7] In fact, the trumpet referred to here is none other than that seventh and last trumpet of the book of Revelation, whose six predecessors sound off throughout the tribulation period:

### Revelation 11:15-18
**And the seventh angel sounded;** and there were great voices in heaven, saying, The kingdoms of this world are become the kingdoms of our Lord, and of his Christ; and he shall reign for ever and ever. And the four and twenty elders, which sat before God on their seats, fell upon their faces, and worshipped God, Saying, We give thee thanks, O Lord God Almighty, which art, and was, and art to come; because thou hast taken to thee thy great power, and hast reigned. **And the nations were angry, and thy wrath is come, and the time of the dead, that they should be judged, and that thou shouldest give reward unto thy servants the prophets, and to the saints, and them that fear thy name, small and great**; and shouldest destroy them which destroy the earth.

The "dead" that are to be judged in this seventh trumpet passage are the dead in Christ that shall rise first at his

---

7   See also 2 Thessalonians 2:1-12 regarding Paul's admonition against those who teach a pre-tribulation gathering of saints doctrine.

coming, which is further described in the three passages below:

### 1 Corinthians 15:51-53

Behold, I shew you a mystery; We shall not all sleep, but we shall all be changed, in a moment, in the twinkling of an eye, **at the last trump:**[8] **for the trumpet will sound, and the dead shall be raised incorruptible, and we shall be changed.** For this corruptible must put on incorruption, and this mortal must put on immortality.

### 1 Thessalonians 4:15-17

For this we say unto you by the word of the Lord, that we which are alive and remain unto the coming of the Lord shall not prevent them which are asleep. For the Lord himself shall descend from heaven with a shout, with the voice of the archangel, and with the **trump of God:** and the **dead in Christ shall rise first:** Then we which are alive and remain shall be caught up together with them in the clouds, to meet the Lord in the air: and so shall we ever be with the Lord.

### Revelation 20:4-5

And I saw thrones, and they sat upon them, and judgment was given unto them: and I saw the souls of them that were beheaded for the witness of Jesus, and for the word of God, and which had not worshipped the beast, neither his image, neither had received his mark upon their foreheads, or in their hands; and they lived and reigned with Christ a thousand years. But the rest of the dead lived not again until the thousand years were finished. **This is the first resurrection.**[9]

---

[8]  This implies that this trumpet is the last within a series of trumpets. Compare Revelation 8:2 & 8:6.

[9]  In seeing that this is the first resurrection, the notion of a pre-tribulation rapture is here proven to be all the more false.

In this last passage, notice the exclusive nature of the first resurrection, for it is limited to Tribulation Saints.

Nonetheless, at the LORD's coming, and with the armies of heaven following after him, the armies of Satan, the Beast, and the False Prophet will be engaged, defeated, and slain with the sword that proceeds out of the mouth of the Word of God. All the fowls of the earth will be filled with their flesh. However, the Beast and the False Prophet will be captured and cast into a lake of fire burning with brimstone to be tormented forever. Satan will be bound and cast into the Bottomless Pit, where he will be imprisoned for one thousand years (see Revelation 19:11, 20:1-3). This battle is the first of two Gog and Magog battles, of which a detailed account can be found in Ezekiel 39. The second Gog and Magog war will occur after a thousand years of peace have been accomplished (Revelation 20:7-10, Ezekiel 38).

## The Millennial Reign of Christ

Once the dust from the Great War has settled, and all is calm again, the day that the prophets and saints have yearned for will have finally arrived. Yahushua Hamashiac (Jesus Christ)—the Word of God incarnate—will reign in Zion, as it is written according to the prophet:

> **Unto us a son is given: and the government shall be upon his shoulder: and his name shall be called Wonderful Counseller, the Mighty God, The Everlasting Father, The Prince of Peace. Of the increase of his government and peace there shall be no end, upon the throne of David, and upon his kingdom, to order it, and to establish it with judgment and with justice from**

**henceforth even for ever. The zeal of the Lord of Host will perform this. (Isaiah 9:7)**

Again, Isaiah states,

**And it shall come to pass in the last days, that the mountain of the Lord's house shall be established in the top of the mountains, and shall be exalted above the hills; and all nations shall flow unto it. And many people shall go and say, Come ye, and let us go up to the mountain of the Lord, to the house of the God of Jacob; and he will teach us of his ways, and we will walk in his paths: for out of Zion shall go forth the Law, and the word of the Lord from Jerusalem. And he shall judge among the nations, and shall rebuke many people: and they shall beat their swords into plowshares, and their spears into pruninghooks: nation shall not lift up sword against nation, neither shall they learn war any more. (Isaiah 2:2-4)**

## Gog and Magog Part 2

After Christ's millennial reign of peace, and as a final trial for humanity, God will allow Satan to be released from his prison. And like a hardened and unrepentant criminal, Satan then *"shall go out to deceive the nations which are in the four quarters of the earth, Gog and Magog, to gather them to battle: the number of whom is as the sand of the sea"* (Revelation 20:7-8). They shall make their way even unto Jerusalem, where Satan and his adherents will be defeated once and for all by the terrible judgments that will issue forth from the God of Heaven (see Ezekiel 38:21-22, Revelation 20:9). For his lot, Satan will be *"cast into the lake of fire and brimstone, where the Beast and False Prophet are, and shall be tormented day and night for ever and ever"* (Revelation 20:10).

## Judgement Day

Following this last battle between good and evil, the Day of Judgment will come, and of this day, Scripture says the following:

> **And I saw the dead, small and great, stand before God; and the books were opened: and another book was opened, which is the Book of Life: and the dead were judged out of those things which were written in the books, according to their works. And the sea gave up the dead which were in it; and death and hell delivered up the dead which were in them: and they were judged every man according to their works. And Death and Hell were cast into the lake of fire. This is the second death.   And whosoever was not found written in the Book of Life was cast into the lake of fire (Revelation 20:11-15).**

## A New Heaven and a New Earth

Once Christ has gotten the victory over all things, including death, Scripture says the following regarding our place in the new Heaven and the new Earth:

> **And I saw a new heaven and a new earth: for the first heaven and the first earth were passed away; and there was no more sea. And I John saw the holy city, new**

Jerusalem, coming down from God out of heaven, prepared as a bride adorned for her husband. And I heard a great voice out of heaven saying, Behold, the tabernacle of God is with men, and he will dwell with them, and they shall be his people, and God himself shall be with them, and be their God. And God shall wipe away all tears from their eyes; and there shall be no more death, neither sorrow, nor crying, neither shall there be any more pain: for the former things are passed away. (Revelation 21:1-4)

# CHAPTER 5
## What Is To Be Done Now?

Now that you have a good idea of some things to come regarding the Black Israelite Exodus at the end of this present age, the pressing question is, what should one do to prepare for such events? This chapter is dedicated to giving a few reasonable pointers regarding this topic.

1. Because King Solomon prayed on our behalf if we had ever found ourselves in captivity, we should meet the requirements of his prayer both individually and collectively, which are as follows:

> **If they [Israel] sin against thee, (for there is no man that sins not,) and you be angry with them, and deliver them to the enemy, so that they carry them away captives unto the land of the enemy, far or near; Yet if they shall bethink themselves in the land where they were carried captives, and repent, and make supplication unto thee in the land of them that carried them captives, saying, We have sinned, and have done perversely, we have committed wickedness; And so return unto thee with all their heart, and with all their soul, in the land of their enemies, which led them away captive, and pray unto thee toward their land, which you gave unto their fathers, the city which you have chosen, and the house[1] which I have built for thy name: Then hear you their prayer and their supplication in heaven thy dwelling**

---

[1] Because the Muslim Dome of the Rock stands on the Temple Mount, we should not pay respect to it as we pray toward our land.

**place, and maintain their cause... (1 Kings 8:46-49)**

We need to humble ourselves, pray, seek God's face, and turn from our wicked ways so that YAH (God) might hear from heaven, forgive our sins, and heal our land, as He said He would (2 Chronicles 7:14).[2]

2. Get to know the life and ministry of Jesus Christ (Yahushua Hamashiac), the Son of the living God, by reading through the Gospels of Matthew, Mark, Luke, and John. Next, I would encourage you to embrace Yahushua as your Lord and Savior for the remission of sins and to receive the gift of eternal life available to all who trust in his name. "Neither is there salvation in any other: for there is none other name under heaven given among men, whereby we must be saved" (Acts 4:12).

**For God so loved the world, that he gave his only begotten Son, that whosoever believe in him should not perish, but have everlasting life. For God sent not his Son into the world to condemn the world; but that the world through him might be saved. He that believe on him is not condemned: but he that believes not is condemned already, because he has not believed in the name of the only begotten Son of God. (John 3:16-18)**

3. Attempt to read the Bible thoroughly from Genesis to Revelation as many times as possible. It is your history, guide, and path to truth and light amidst this world of great darkness and falsehood. Study the Bible daily.

---

[2] One of the most profound examples of repentance while in exile can be seen in the example of Daniel the prophet (Daniel 9:2-19).

4. Diligently search out the truth of this book for yourself. Doing this will enable you to stand on a solid foundation and know with certainty that you are indeed an Israelite destined to return to your ancient homeland of Israel to await the coming of the Lord Jesus Christ.

5. Be watchful and alert concerning world affairs and current events and compare them to Bible prophecy. Be ready to move when YAH (God) gives clear orders to do so through his prophets, apostles, saints, and His Holy Spirit. However, until such clear orders are issued, **strengthen yourself, your house, and your community.**

6. Seek out the congregation of the saints and join them, but beware of false teachers and doctrines, for Scripture says: *"There were false prophets also among the people, even as there shall be false teachers among you, who privily [privately] shall bring in damnable heresies, even denying the Lord that bought them, and bring upon themselves swift destruction. And many shall follow their pernicious ways; by reason of whom the way of truth shall be evil spoken of. And through covetousness shall with feigned words make merchandise of you: whose judgment now of a long time lingereth not, and their damnation slumbereth not"* (2Peter 2:1-3).

Note: Beware of the Hebrew Israelites who deny Christ's miraculous birth of a virgin, who are hostile towards the Gentiles in their preaching of the Gospel, and who circulate in our midst a false "Twelve Tribes of Israel" chart. Knowing the Bible for your self is of great importance.

7. *"Go ye therefore, and teach all nations, baptizing them in the name of the Father, and of the Son, and of the Holy Ghost: Teaching them to observe all things whatsoever I [Jesus] have commanded you"* (Matthew 28:19-20). Furthermore, now that you are aware of The Black Israelite Exodus and the End of the Age, spread its message to the lost members of the Nation of Israel dispersed in the Israelite Diaspora.

# SUPPLEMENTS

# The Mystery of Iniquity Revealed

## Part 1: Satan In Heaven As the Accuser

*Now there was a day when the sons of God came to present themselves before the Lord, and Satan came also among them. And the Lord said unto Satan, Whence comest thou? Then Satan answered the Lord, and said, From going to and fro in the earth, and from walking up and down it. And the Lord said unto Satan, Hast thou considered my servant Job, that there is none like him in the earth, a perfect and an upright man, one that feareth God, and escheweth evil? Then Satan answered the Lord, and said, Doth Job fear God for nought? Hast not thou made an hedge about him, and about his house, and about all that he hath on every side? Thou hast blessed the work of his hands, and his substance is increased in the land. But put forth thine hand now, and touch all that he hath, and he will curse thee to thy face. (**Job 1:6-11**)*

---

*Yet Michael the archangel, when contending with the devil he disputed about the body of Moses, dare not bring against him a railing accusation, but said, The Lord rebuke thee. (**Jude v. 9**)*

---

*And he shewed me Joshua the high priest standing before the angel of the Lord, and Satan standing at his right hand to resist him. And the Lord said unto Satan, The Lord rebuke thee, O Satan; even the Lord that hath chosen Jerusalem rebuke thee: is not this a brand plucked out of the fire? (**Zechariah 3:1-2**)*

# Satan Is the god of This World

*And the devil, taking him [Jesus] up into an high mountain, shewed unto him all the kingdoms of the world in a moment of time. And the devil said unto him, All this power will I give thee, and the glory of them: for that is delivered unto me; and to whomsoever I will I give it. If thou therefore wilt worship me, all shall be thine. (Luke 4:5-7)*

## Part 2: Mystery Babylon Revealed (Revelation 17)

### Point #1
The Seven Heads on which the woman sits represent two things:   **1)** Seven Mountains and **2)** Seven Kings (Rev. 17:9-10). Because of the common symbol (seven heads) that the seven mountains and seven kings share, one can perceive that a relationship exists between the mountains and the kings. The nature of the relationship is that each of the seven mountains is ruled by a king identified with it, so that Mountain 1 is ruled by King 1, Mountain 2 by King 2, et cetera.

### Point #2
The statement *"five are fallen, one is, and the other is not yet come"* (Rev. 17:10) regarding the seven kings is one that shows that all seven kings DO NOT reign at the same time. Moreover, because each king is connected to one of the seven mountains on which the woman sits, we can conclude that the seven mountains DO NOT exist at the same time either.

### Point #3
In Revelation 17, we find the woman (whore) sitting on **a)** many waters (v. 1) and on **b)** seven mountains (v. 9).

These two descriptions of what the woman is seated upon represent different ways of looking at essentially the same thing. Deriving from Revelation 17:15 and 17:18, the waters represent peoples, multitudes, nations, and tongues that the woman (Mystery Babylon) reigns over. Likewise, each of the seven mountains, which DO NOT exist concurrently, represents a kingdom whose king has rule over the peoples, multitudes, nations, and tongues of the earth. To validate this last point, understand the following three things: First, the same way in which the book of Daniel uses a mountain to represent a kingdom (Daniel 2:35, 44-45) is the same way in which it is used here. Secondly, the seventh king who rules the seventh mountain or kingdom is the same as the first beast in Revelation 13:1-8 and that *"power was given him over ALL kindreds, and tongues, and nations"* (Revelation 13:7; also compare Rev. 13:3 & Rev. 17:8). Third and last, the six kings preceding this seventh king enjoyed equally the same type of powerful crown or kingdom that the seventh king will have at his coming. Read:

> "And there appeared another wonder in heaven; and behold a great red dragon, having seven heads and ten horns, AND SEVEN CROWNS UPON HIS HEADS" (Revelation 12:3).

Again, the seven mountains, which DO NOT exist concurrently, represent a kingdom whose king has rule over the peoples, multitudes, nations, and tongues of the earth.

### Point #4
At the same time in which the Sixth King (the king who IS, Revelation 17:10) has rule over all kindreds, tongues, and nations, we find that the Harlot (Mystery Babylon) has rule over the peoples, multitudes, nations, and tongues as well (Revelation 17:15). But how can this be? How can the

Sixth King AND Mystery Babylon reign over all the earth's inhabitants at the exact same time? Easily, for simple logic says that Mystery Babylon and the kingdom of the Sixth King are both one and the same.

## Point #5

"And he cried mightily with a strong voice, saying, Babylon the great is fallen, is fallen..." (Revelation 18:2)

With the coming of the Seventh King and his kingdom, the sixth Babylonian kingdom will join the ranks of the first five who have "fallen." But will the fall of Mystery Babylon as the Sixth head of the Beast be the end of the BABYLONIAN SYSTEM? Not at all! Remember that the woman (Mystery Babylon) sits on all seven heads (kingdoms), not just the sixth one (Revelation 17:9) and that all seven kingdoms emerge consecutively at different points in time. And just like the Sixth kingdom of the beast has the blasphemous name of *"Mystery Babylon, The Mother of Harlots and Abominations of the Earth"* written on its forehead by the mere fact that the Sixth Kingdom and Mystery Babylon are one and the same, the other kingdoms have the same name written across their forehead. Read: *"And I stood upon the sand of the sea, and saw a beast rise up out of the sea, having seven heads and ten horns, and upon his horns ten crowns, and UPON HIS HEADS THE NAME OF BLASPHEMY"* (Revelation 13:1). Notice that all seven heads have one name in common. And since Mystery Babylon is the Sixth head of the beast and her name is revealed, we know the blasphemous name of the other heads—MYSTERY BABYLON THE GREAT, THE MOTHER OF HARLOTS AND ABOMINATIONS OF THE EARTH. Hence, there are seven different manifestations of Mystery Babylon, in which the seventh manifestation and its king have not yet come.

## Point #6

The question that now arises is, what kingdoms represent the seven manifestations of Mystery Babylon? The scriptures give us the answer in part to this question. By studying Daniel's interpretation of Nebuchadnezzar's dream concerning the statue (Daniel 2:31-45), along with his vision of the four beasts (Daniel 7), and by linking these up with Revelation 13 and 17, we know that the beast with seven heads and ten horns first began to manifest itself after Babylon, Media/Persia and Greece had all fallen as consecutive rulers of the world. The next nation to rule the world were the Romans. Now, there is a tendency here to see Rome as THE beastly kingdom with seven heads and ten horns, but that would be a huge mistake. Instead, one should view Rome as the FIRST head of seven Mystery Babylonian superpowers, which collectively constitute the Fourth Kingdom of the book of Daniel (7:7). The ruler of this Fourth Kingdom is Satan, who gives power to seven different kings at different points in time until the end. Nonetheless, to figure out the remaining six manifestations of Mystery Babylon, one must study what kingdoms emerged AFTER Rome (not before) that had or currently has dominion over the kings of the earth, which is a key characteristic of Mystery Babylon:

> And the woman which thou sawest is that great city, which reigneth over the kings of the earth. (Revelation 17:18)

Mystery Babylon number six, along with its sixth king, is presented in the book of Revelation within the context of the Great Tribulation going head to head in battle with the final Mystery Babylonian kingdom (Rev. 17:16); and by the time this period occurs, five previous kingdoms (heads) would have fallen (Rev. 17:10).

At the coming of the seventh king (Antichrist/the Beast), he will establish his seat at Jerusalem, making it the temporary headquarters of the final Mystery Babylonian empire. Accompanying the Antichrist will be a ten-king alliance from the following "Middle Eastern" nations outlined in Psalm 83:

1. Edom, 2. Ishmaelites, 3. Moab 4. Hagarenes 5. Gebal 6. Ammon 7. Amalek 8. Philistines 9. Tyre 10. Assur

These will "consult together with one consent" (Psalm 83:5) and will "have one mind, and shall give their power and strength unto the beast" (Revelation 17:13). Three of the kings from this alliance will be plucked up by Antichrist (Daniel 7:8), making him the eighth king of this group. All in all, Antichrist is the seventh head or king of the seven-headed beast, and he is the eighth and primary ruler of those kings who will rule with him once he takes down three of the original ten (Revelation 17:11).

## Point #7
From the time when Rome replaced Greece as the world's most dominant superpower up to the dominant superpower ruling even at this time, the world has been ruled by Satan, his angels, and by the kings who have accepted the kingdoms that Jesus rejected during the days of his temptation (Luke 4:5-7). Through Satan's agents that run the most powerful governments, the Mystery Babylonian System has been maintained to wage constant war against God's saints and systematically set the stage for the world to worship Satan and his seventh king as God (Revelation 13:4). The seat of this seventh king will be located at Jerusalem, where he will sit in the very Temple of God, haughtily showing himself that he is God (2 Thessalonians 2:4).

# From Babylon to the Antichrist: 10 Dominant World Superpowers
*Based on the Visions of Daniel & the Revelation of John

Nebuchadnezzar

Cyrus

Alexander

Satan

Babylon
(Lion)

Medo–Persia
(Bear)

Greece
(Leopard with 4 Heads)

Mystery Babylon
(Dragon with 7 Heads
and 10 Horns)

SEVEN SUPERPOWERS

Head 1 (Fallen)      Head 5 (Fallen)
Head 2 (Fallen)      Head 6 (IS)
Head 3 (Fallen)      Head 7 + 10 horns (Yet to come)
Head 4 (Fallen)

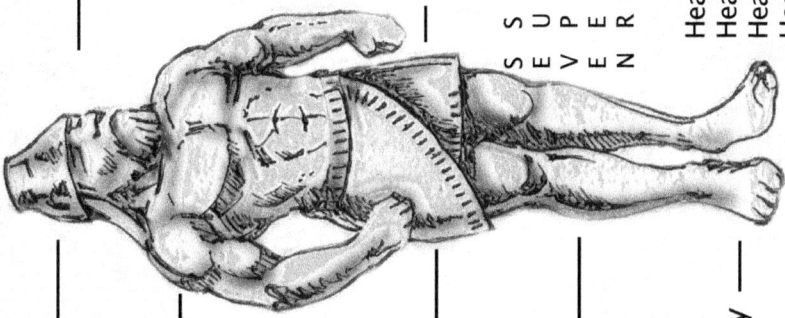

Gold ——

Silver ——

Brass ——

Iron ——

Iron & Clay ——

But just as the six kingdoms before the seventh one were and will be made to fall, the seventh beastly kingdom will be destroyed at the glorious coming of our Lord and Saviour Jesus Christ (Revelation 19:11-21). He will set up a kingdom that shall indeed remain forever (Daniel 2:44). However, until our Lord returns, know that we as true Christians *"wrestle not against flesh and blood, but against principalities, against powers, against the rulers of the darkness of this world, against spiritual wickedness in high places"* (Ephesians 6:12).

## Part 3: The United States of America— The Current Head of the Beast

From the inception of America to the present, many of her ruling elite have been secretly promoting Satan's 666 agenda to condition the world into rebelling against Yah (God) and worship Satan and his Antichrist instead:

> And all the world wondered after the beast. And they worshipped the dragon which gave power unto the beast: and they worshipped the beast... (Rev. 13:3-4)

And now that the United States of America reigns over the kings of the earth,[1] she (the current Mystery Babylon) promotes this Satanic agenda like never before. To prove that America indeed has this agenda in place, let us analyze carefully the very seal that America has been using to represent herself, which can be seen on the back of the U.S. One Dollar Bill.

---

[1] New York City, the headquarters of the United Nations.

## AONMS = MASON
(Ancient Order Nobles Mystic Shrine)

By superimposing a triangle onto the pyramid of the U.S. seal to form a hexagram or what some might call "Solomon's Seal," which also can be seen above the eagle's head, the secret and satanic religion of Freemasonry is revealed. Through signs, symbols, and decoding methods like these, Freemasonry's evil agenda is communicated to its initiates.

At the base of the pyramid, the following letters are displayed: MDCCLXXVI. When added up, these letters are the Roman numerical equivalent of 1776—the year in which the U.S. declared independence from Britain.

| | | |
|---|---|---|
| **M**-1000 | **C**-100 | **X**-10 |
| **D**-500 | **L**-50 | **V**-5 |
| **C**-100 | **X**-10 | **I**-1 |

(1776)

However, when arranged in the following scheme using the pyramid and its base as a key, the infamous number of the name of the Beast (666) is unveiled:

| 1000 | 100 | 10 |
| M | C | X |

| D-500 | 600 | 100-C | L-50 | 60 | 10-X | V-5 | 6 | 1-I |
|---|---|---|---|---|---|---|---|---|
| (Six Hundred) | | | (Threescore) | | | (Six) | | |

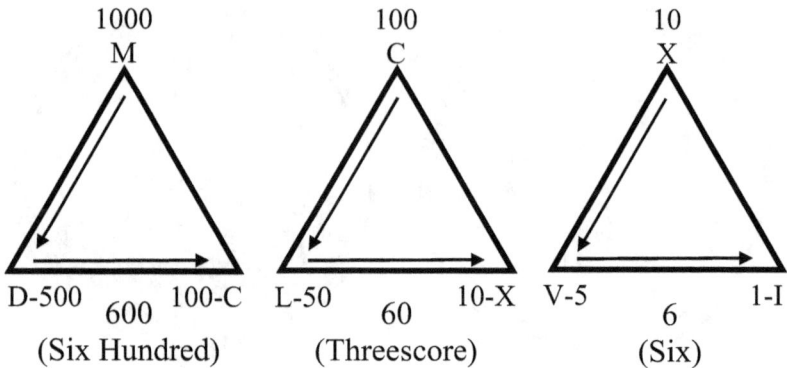

And he causeth all, both small and great, rich and poor, free and bond, to receive a mark in their right hand, or in their foreheads: And that no man might buy or sell, save he that had the mark, or the name of the beast, or the number of his name. Here is wisdom, Let him that hath understanding count the number of the beast: for it is the number of a man; and his number is Six hundred threescore and six. (Revelation 13:16-18)

Think not that deciphering the U.S. seal to reveal the Beast's number is only a mere coincidence. Instead, it is a telltale sign of who really is in charge of America and the agenda being pushed. The United States "IS" the 6th kingdom that we find in Revelation (17:10). She is fulfilling her role within a seven-stage process of being at war with the saints of God and conditioning the world spiritually into accepting the Antichrist (the beast) upon his arrival.

## Part 4: The Accuser of the Brethren is Cast Down & The Arrival of the 7th King

*And there was war in heaven: Michael and his angels fought against the dragon; and the dragon fought and his* angels, and prevailed not; neither was their place found any more in heaven. And the great dragon was cast out, that old serpent, called the Devil, and Satan, which deceiveth the whole world: he was cast out into the earth, and his angels were cast out with him. And I heard a loud voice saying in heaven, Now is come salvation, and strength, and the kingdom of our God, and the power of his Christ: for the accuser of our brethren is cast down, which accused them before our God day and night. And they overcame him by the blood of the Lamb, and by the word of their testimony; and they loved not their lives unto the death. Therefore rejoice, ye heavens, and ye that dwell in them. Woe to the inhabiters of the earth and of the sea! For the devil is come down unto you, having great wrath, because he knoweth that he hath but a short time. *(Revelation 12:7-12)*

And the fifth angel sounded, and I saw a star fall from heaven unto the earth: and to him was given the key of the bottomless pit. And he opened the bottomless pit; and there arose a smoke out of the pit, as the smoke of a great furnace; and the sun and the air were darkened by reason of the smoke of the pit. And there came out of the smoke locusts upon the earth: and unto them was given power, as the scorpions of the earth have power... And they had a king over them, which is the angel of the bottomless pit, whose name in the Hebrew tongue is Abaddon, but in the Greek tongue hath his name Apollyon. *(Revelation 9:1-11)*

And I saw one of his heads as it were wounded to death; and his deadly wound was healed: and all the world wondered after the beast. And they worshipped the dragon which gave power unto the beast: and they worshipped the beast, saying, Who is like unto the beast? Who is able to make war with him? *(Revelation 13:3-4)*

# Louis Farrakhan's (The False Christ) Savior's Day 2010 Speech: "The Wheel" (last 13 min)

"Well now, I'm a say this and go: What did Paul mean, 'I have kept the faith, I have fought the good fight, I have finished my course, and now is laid up for me a crown of righteousness and I go that that great judge of righteousness will give that crown, and it's not only for me but it's for us who love his appearance.'

I came here tonight to tell you that that one more thing that I had to do, I started the process of doing it today. They'll be angry with me, and I will be betrayed into their hands. And some of you Muslims that think I'm trying to set something up that don't have to happen, you not gone make the prophets liars. Somebody got to fulfill it. See, Jesus was a good man but they charged him with blasphemy and then they charged him with sedition. I'm ready to do whatever God has for me to do. And the United States government, you can do whatever you want to do with me, and don't spare me. Come at me with all your power. And I want to prove to you that I am with God and God is with me and there is nothing that you can do to me, except what pleases God. I'm on my way to my father, but I will return. It ain't no death for me. Not now. I'm going to get the next lesson. But while I'm gone: war, revolution, bloodshed. Allah will never reveal the new wisdom while the wicked have power. So when you hear that the minister is gone, and some of you will see me—go. They said they saw him go up in a cloud, and he'll come back in like manner. When you see me again, I'll be a brand new man. When you see me again, I can show you my sides that have been pierced; where they took my organs, doctors who thought they would get rid of me, but I'm alive. And when you see me again, you'll know that I've been in the presence of God."

# Book of Revelation
# Tribulation Overview

## *The Seven Seals (Revelation 6-8:1)*

**1.** *White Horse*: He that sat on him had a bow; and a crown was given unto him: and he went forth conquering and to conquer.

**2.** *Red Horse*: Power was given to him that sat thereon to take peace from the earth, and that they should kill one another: and there was given unto him a great sword.

**3.** *Black Horse*: He that sat on him had a pair of balances in his hand (A measure of wheat for a penny, and three measures of barley for a penny; and see thou hurt not the oil and the wine)

**4.** *Pale Horse*: His name that sat on him was Death, and Hell followed with him. Power was given unto them over the fourth part of the earth, to kill with the sword, and with hunger, and with death, and with the beasts of the earth.

**5.** a) Souls under the altar who were slain for the word of God and their testimony b) cried saying "How long do you not judge and avenge our blood c) white robes given to them and were told to rest for a little season until their fellow servants and brothers to be killed as they were was fulfilled.

**6.** Earthquake, Sun Blackened, Blood Moon, Stars fall, **Heaven departs as a scroll**, Every mountain and island moved out of their places, kings, great men, rich and poor, captains, mighty men, bond and free men, hid themselves saying to the mountains and rocks, "hide us from the face of him on the throne and from the wrath of the Lamb: For the great day of his wrath is come; and who shall be able to stand?"

**7.** Silence in Heaven for about half an hour.

## *The Seven Trumpets (Revelation 8:2-11:19)*

**1.** Hail, fire mingled with blood cast to earth; 1/3 trees burnt and all green grass burnt.

**2.** Great burning mountain cast into the sea, 1/3 sea becomes blood, 1/3 sea creatures die, 1/3 ships destroyed.

**3.** Great Burning star (Wormwood) falls on 1/3 part of rivers and fountains of water. 1/3 part of waters became wormwood. Many men died of the bitter waters.

**4.** 1/3 of sun, moon, and stars smitten so as the 1/3 part of them was darkened, and the day and night shone not for a 1/3 part of it.

### (3 Woes: 5th, 6th, and 7th Trumpets)

**5.** Bottomless Pit opened, Abaddon (Apollyon) and his "locust" army. Hurt not the grass, greenery, or trees, but only those men without the seal of God in their foreheads. Not kill, but torment men for 5 months.

**6.** 4 Angels in the Euphrates loosed to kill 1/3 of man by fire, smoke, and brimstone; (200 Thousand thousand army)Two witnesses killed and ascend. Earthquake (1/10 of Jerusalem fall; 7000 die)

**7.** The Mystery of God is finished. Kingdoms of this world are become of our Lord and of his Christ... Thy wrath is come, and the time of the dead, that they should be judged, and that thou should give reward unto thy servants the prophets, and to the saints, and them that fear thy name, small and great; and should destroy them which destroy the earth. And the Temple of God was opened in heaven, and there was seen in his Temple the Ark of His Testament...

## *The Seven Last Plagues (Vials)* *(Revelation 15-16)*

**1.** Poured out on earth. Noisome and grievous sore upon those with the mark of the beast.

**2.** Poured upon the sea. Sea turned to blood. Everything dies in the sea.

**3.** Poured upon rivers. Rivers, fountains, and waters become blood.

**4.** Poured upon Sun. Power given to the angel to scorch men with fire.

**5.** Poured on the seat of the Beast; and his kingdom is filled with darkness, and they gnawed their tongues for pain and blasphemed.

**6.** Poured on the Euphrates. The Euphrates dried up. Kings of the East gathered at Armageddon.

**7.** Poured into the air. It is done. Unparalleled Great Earthquake, the Great City divided into three parts, Cities of the nations fall. Every island and mountain flees. Babylon is judged. Plague of hail.

www.ingramcontent.com/pod-product-compliance
Lightning Source LLC
LaVergne TN
LVHW021537080426
835509LV00019B/2685